TOYS and PLAY

with everyday materials

Sudarshan Khanna | Gita Wolf | Anushka Ravishankar | Priya Sundram

HAVE YOU EVER MADE YOUR OWN TOYS?

It's really not difficult. Children in the past used to play with toys they made themselves. In India, there were also toymakers in villages and small towns who made wonderfully clever toys from simple everyday material. They didn't cost very much, and they were very different from anything you can buy in the shops today. For one, no toy looked like another— each had been individually made and was therefore very unique. They were very simply but intelligently put together. Sadly, you can no longer find these playthings, or the people who make them.

It would be a great pity if these wonderful ideas were to disappear completely, so we've put together this book which shows you how to make some of these toys, using everyday material you find around you. While most of them are very easy to make if you follow the instructions in the book, in some cases you might need the help of an adult.

All the toys you see in this book were made by a group of children. There's another interesting thing about them: even though they look simple, it's fascinating to find out how and why they work in the way they do; so we've also tried to explain the science behind some of the toys. We don't normally think of toymakers as scientists or technical people, but actually they are a little like scientists: they experiment a lot with different materials and ways of putting them together. And through trial and error, they then arrive at the final form of a toy.

You could go through the science sections on your own, or ask an adult to explain things to you. In any case, when you make a toy you will discover many other things along the way: how materials feel and behave, what to think about when your toy doesn't do what it is supposed to, and what fun it is when it does. So, in a sense, you will be both toymaker and scientist!

IF YOU'RE A PARENT OR EDUCATOR

The toys in this book were developed by Professor Sudarshan Khanna, India's best known toy researcher and designer. He recollects that as a child, he knew how to make at least a dozen toys, but these ideas have all but disappeared today. His interest in folk toys has taken him around small villages and towns in India over a period of almost four decades, to find toymakers who made the most creative and intelligent use of simple everyday materials to create wonderful playthings. He documented these traditions, and continued to develop their design principles, coming up with more than 150 toys in the process. To revive this lost art, he conducted workshops with children, teachers and toymakers, guiding them through the process of re-creating a remarkable tradition.

We asked him to hold a workshop with Tara Books, along with a group of children, and this book came out of that encounter. During the workshops, we noticed how children of different age groups reacted not only to the experience of making their own toys, but also to the way they played with them. This quality of play was very special, and set us thinking: can today's children, who are surrounded by so many toys and gadgets, still play in a freewheeling, unstructured way? How do particular toys determine the nature of play? We decided to explore these concerns in some depth, and came up with the second part of this book. This comprises short essays on the idea and importance of play.

CONTENTS

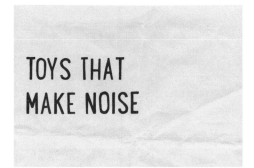

TOYS THAT MAKE NOISE

Flute-hoot 20

Twist 30

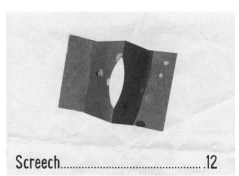

Buzz 10

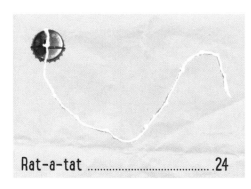

Hum 22

Hip-hop 33

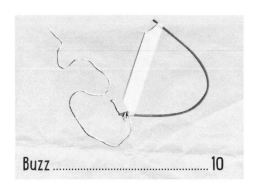

Screech 12

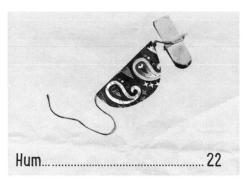

Rat-a-tat 24

Rock-n-roll 35

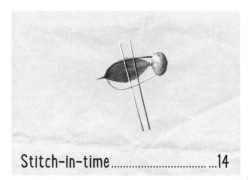

Stitch-in-time 14

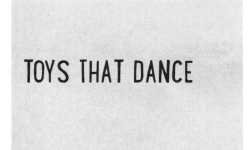

TOYS THAT DANCE

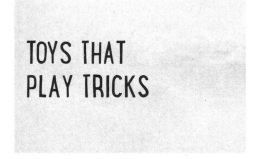

TOYS THAT PLAY TRICKS

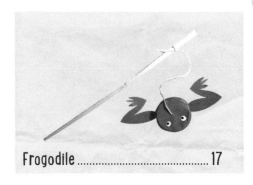

Frogodile 17

Jitter-bug 28

Clap-trap 40

Flower-power................................42

Pop-up......................................45

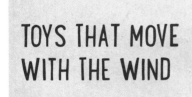

TOYS THAT MOVE
WITH THE WIND

Retpocileh................................50

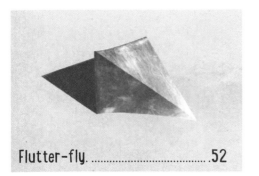

Flutter-fly................................52

Spinning Sardine........................54

Naf...56

TOYS THAT
NEED SKILL

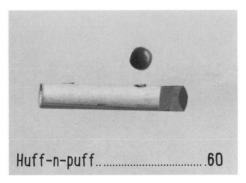

Huff-n-puff..............................60

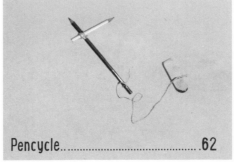

Pencycle..................................62

Yankee....................................64

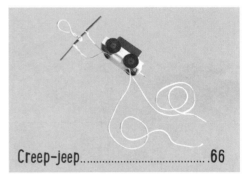

Creep-jeep...............................66

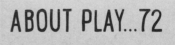
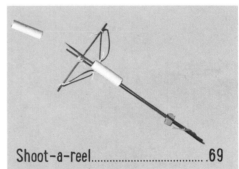

Shoot-a-reel.............................69

ABOUT PLAY...72

Reflections • Folk Toys • Tradition
• Material • Own Toys • Short-lived
Toys • Process and Product • Dare
to be Different • True Interaction
• History • Play • Boredom • Stages
of Play • Systems of Play • Good
Toys • Traditional Play • Dolls
• Rules of Game • Violent Toys

Appendix................................112

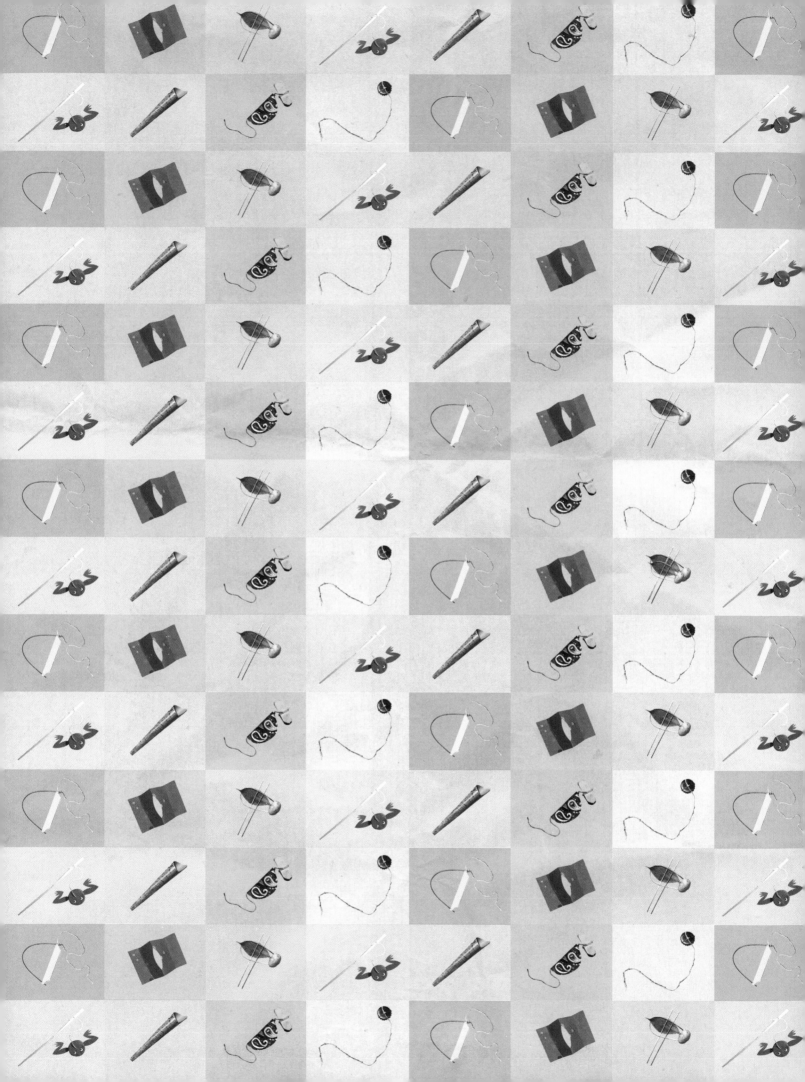

TOYS THAT MAKE NOISE

Buzz

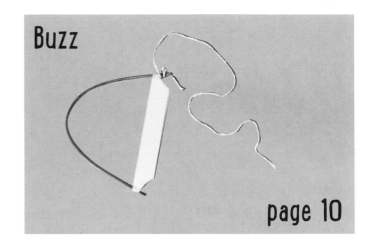

page 10

Screech

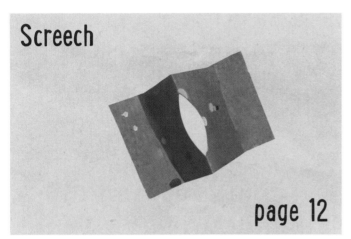

page 12

Stitch-in-time

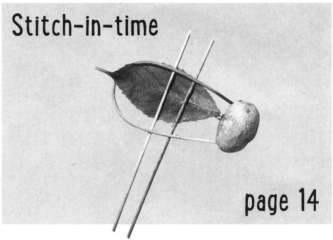

page 14

Frogodile

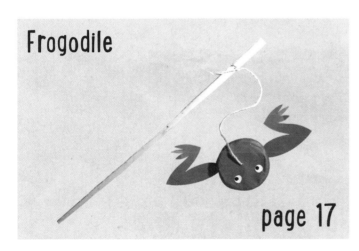

page 17

Flute-hoot

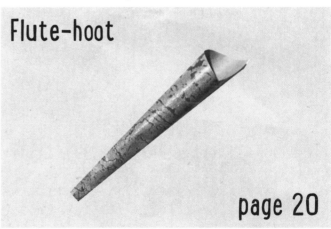

page 20

Hum

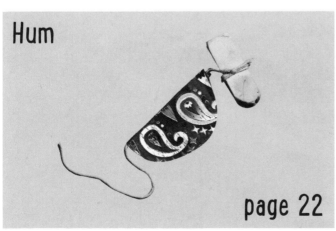

page 22

Rat-a-tat

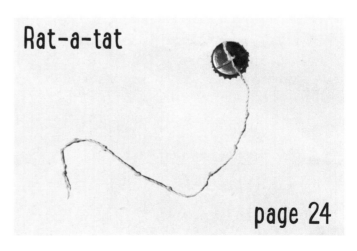

page 24

Buzz

Buzzbuzzbuzzbuzz
That is what
Buzz does.

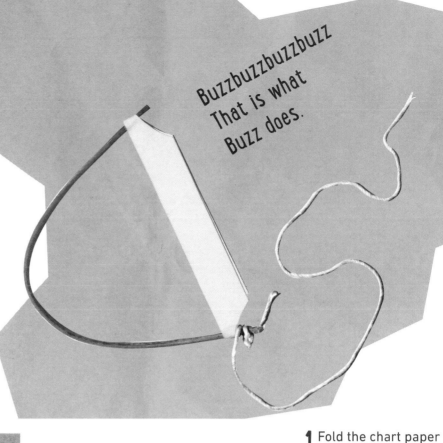

You will need

+ a strip of chart paper, 25 x 2 cm
+ a thin, flexible stick, 20 cm
+ string, 40 to 50 cm

HOW IT IS MADE

1 Fold the chart paper strip in two and glue the open ends together.

2 Cut the two ends of the loop as shown.

3 Bend the stick and glue the two ends to the ends of the loop.

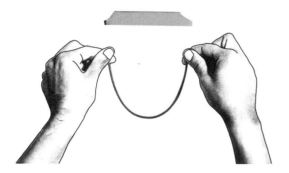

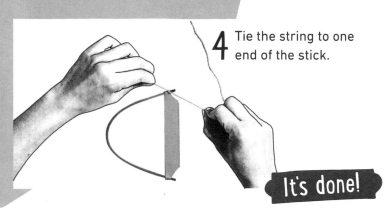

4 Tie the string to one end of the stick.

 It's done!

What it does

Hold the end of the string and swing it round swiftly. The Buzz will buzz.

When it doesn't

Try swinging it faster. If it still doesn't buzz, check:

- if the stick is too flexible,
- if the flaps are jammed together.

Buzz, Buzzer, Buzzest

Make all your friends stand in a row. Each of you swing your Buzz as fast as you can, and choose a winner.
The winner can be chosen in different ways:

1. Whose Buzz is the loudest?
2. Whose Buzz has the highest (or lowest) pitch?
3. Whose expression is the funniest, as they swing the Buzz?
4. Who manages to swing it for the longest time without hitting anyone with it?

And so on.

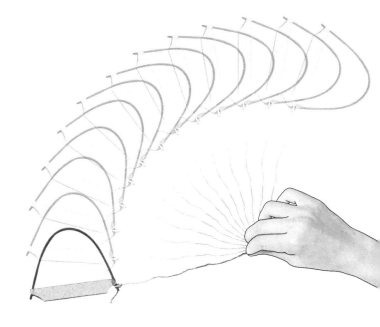

Frequency of Sound

Sounds are vibrations of the air and can be generated by vibrating surfaces or membranes. The Buzz buzzes because the two flaps vibrate against each other.
The bent stick keeps the two flaps in a state of tension. When it is rotated swiftly the tension in the stick causes the flaps to vibrate against each other. The number of vibrations per second is called the frequency of the sound. When the frequency is low, we hear a low buzz. If the frequency is increased the buzz becomes high-pitched.

→ Try

Make a Buzz with different kinds of paper. Try also with leaves. Does each one sound different?

Use a shorter string and a longer string. Does the sound change? Why?

Hint: the sound is louder when air flows faster and in greater amounts between the flaps.

→ Think

Why does the pitch get higher when you spin the Buzz faster and faster?

Hint: the number of vibrations per second depends on the speed of rotation.

Screech

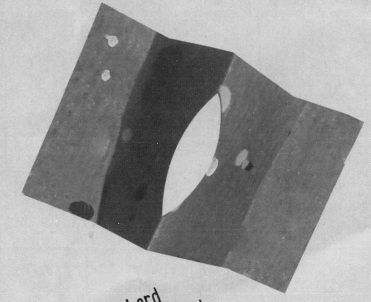

If you blow this long and hard
A screech will be your just reward
(By the way we do beseech
Don't underestimate this Screech).

You will need

+ a piece of paper, 5 x 10 cm
+ scissors

HOW IT IS MADE

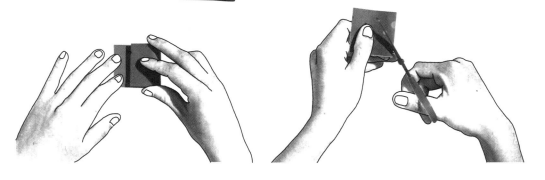

1 Fold the paper in half and cut out a hole in the centre.

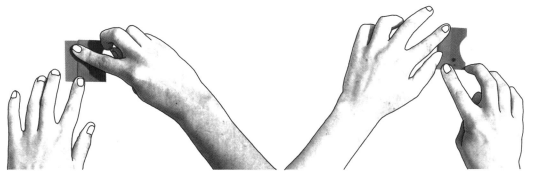

2 Now fold out the two sides as shown.

It's done!

What it does

Hold the whistle between two fingers and blow hard. It might let out a shrill screech like a peacock with a sore throat. Or it might make a nasal noise like an elephant with a cold.

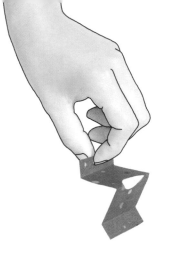

When it doesn't

It usually works. If it doesn't, try holding it differently. Blow harder. If that doesn't help, blow gently. Keep trying. Suddenly, you'll be rewarded with a screech.

SOUND EFFECTS

Need a nice hair-raising scream in your murder-mystery play? Want a good shriek for the peacock in your puppet show? Use the Screech.

13

Stitch-in-time

Can you have a ghost without the dead?
Can you stitch a leaf without a thread?
A Stitch-in-time can do the latter
Though the leaf might end up a-tatter.

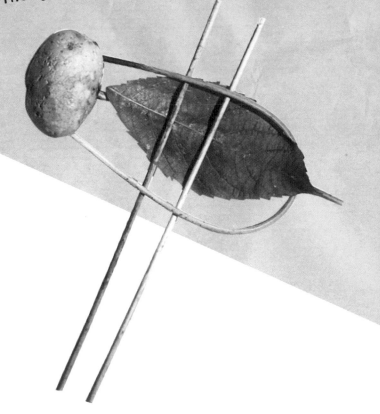

You will need

+ 4 thick broomsticks:
  one 30 cm, one 15 cm and two 20 cm
+ one leaf
+ a small potato

HOW IT IS MADE

1 Sharpen the ends of the 30 cm stick and insert both ends into the potato, forming a loop.

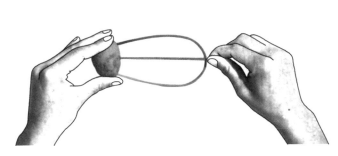

2 Insert the 15 cm stick into the potato, so that it is at the centre of the loop.

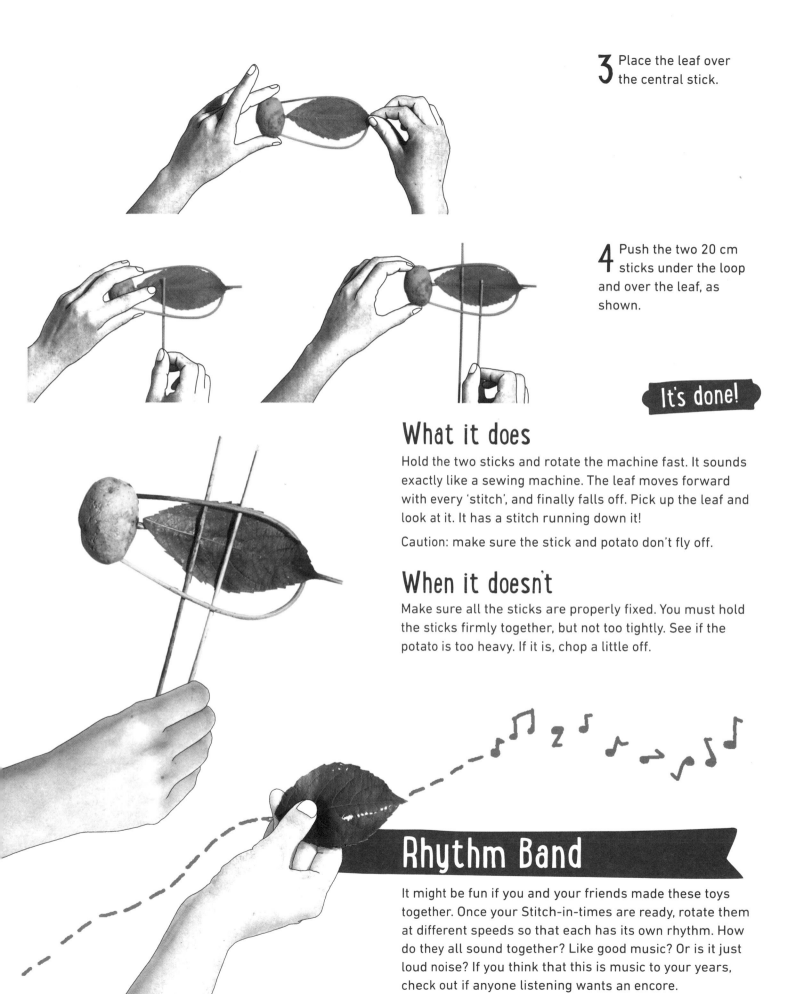

3 Place the leaf over the central stick.

4 Push the two 20 cm sticks under the loop and over the leaf, as shown.

What it does

Hold the two sticks and rotate the machine fast. It sounds exactly like a sewing machine. The leaf moves forward with every 'stitch', and finally falls off. Pick up the leaf and look at it. It has a stitch running down it!

Caution: make sure the stick and potato don't fly off.

When it doesn't

Make sure all the sticks are properly fixed. You must hold the sticks firmly together, but not too tightly. See if the potato is too heavy. If it is, chop a little off.

Rhythm Band

It might be fun if you and your friends made these toys together. Once your Stitch-in-times are ready, rotate them at different speeds so that each has its own rhythm. How do they all sound together? Like good music? Or is it just loud noise? If you think that this is music to your years, check out if anyone listening wants an encore.

Transport Mechanism

The two sticks get twisted and turn around with every rotation. The one that is on top hits the leaf with a sharp tap as it switches places with the one that is below. The force of the tap makes a hole in the leaf. The stick also pushes the leaf forward, creating a transport mechanism which converts the rotation into a forward movement.

→ Try

Would this work with cloth, or even paper? The leaf is soft and easily pierced. Cloth and paper would be able to withstand the force of the stick.

The cloth would muffle the noise, since the sound would get absorbed. The leaf, although it is soft, does not absorb the noise, because it gets cut at that point.

→ Think

The transport mechanism at work in this toy is similar to the mechanism that operates in a conveyor belt. Can you think of other instances where rotation is converted to a forward movement?

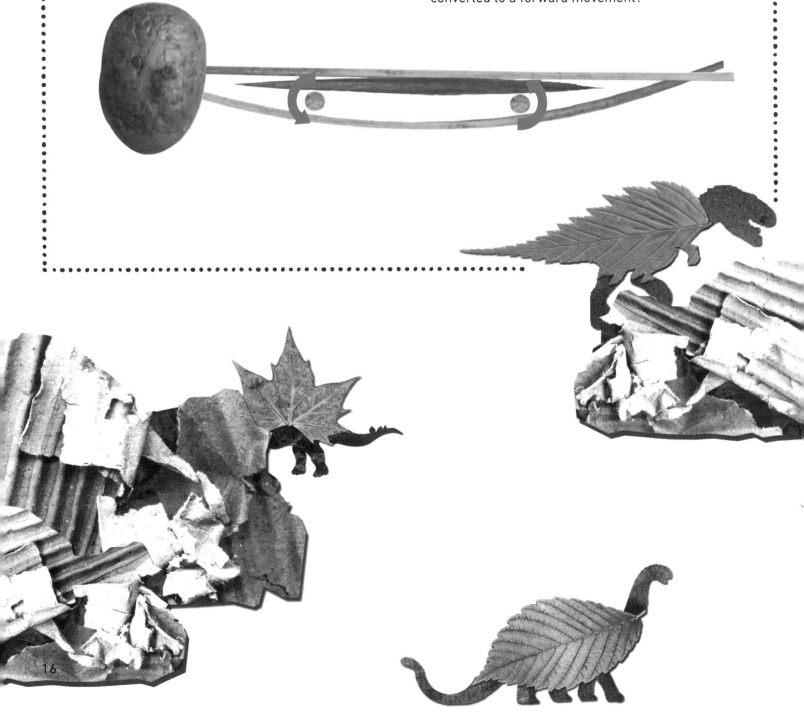

Frogodile

Never smile at a Frogodile
For he's a moody kind of bloke
Keep a straight mug
And mutter "Gugggugg"
Or he might refuse to croak.

You will need

+ thin strong paper, 8 x 8 cm
+ string, 15 cm
+ clay
+ a thick stick, 15 cm
+ a matchstick

HOW IT IS MADE

1 Make a small, shallow clay pot, about 4 cm in diameter. Let it dry completely.

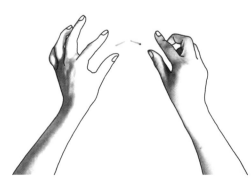

2 Tie a small piece of string to one end of the matchstick.

17

3 Cut out a piece of paper big enough to cover the pot.

4 With a pin, punch a small hole at the centre of the paper and pass the string through it, as shown.

5 Paste the paper over the open end of the pot, with the piece of stick inside and the free end of the string hanging out. The paper should be tightly stretched.

6 Cut a groove in the thick stick and tie the free end of the string loosely around it.

It's done!

What it does

Put a few drops of water at the place where the string is attached to the stick. Meanwhile, mutter the magic words: *Om Gugggugg Shree Tinnavalli.* Swing the drum, using the stick. Your Frogodile will croak.

When it doesn't

Laryngitis? Lost its voice?

Or maybe Gugggugg and Tinnavalli are displeased? While chanting, you have either put too little or too much water.

Have you stuck the paper onto the drum properly? Is the string tied so tight that it has no space to move? This will make it wind around the stick, instead of moving around it. Don't tie it too loosely either, or the drum will fly off the stick.

sound waves

friction

sound

Transmission & Amplification of Sound

The friction between the wet thread and the stick produces a slight sound. The sound travels along the string in the form of waves. This makes the paper surface vibrate and the sound is amplified because of the large surface stretched over the drum.

Why doesn't the Frogodile croak if there is no water? The friction between the two surfaces is usually too slight to cause a croak, but a drop of water makes the string swell, and therefore increases the friction. If you put too much water, the water acts as a lubricant between the string and stick, so there is less friction.

→ Try

Change the length of the string. If the string is longer does the sound get louder or fainter?

Will changing the size of the drum affect the sound? How?

Use paper of varying thickness and see how the sound changes. If you use cloth in place of paper, do you think the Frogodile will croak?

Hint: all materials absorb some sounds and transmit some. Soft materials are good at absorbing sound.

If you get carried away and use many layers of paper, the Frogodile is silenced. Why?

→ Think

Traditionally this toy was made of hair from a horse's tail, and not string. Can you guess the reason for this?

Hint: if you use horse hair, you need not invoke Gugggugg and gang.

Flute-hoot

This is a special flute
It gives a hollow hoot
When it's in the mood

It sounds quite good
And when it's not it's mute.

You will need

+ a piece of paper, 8 x 8 cm
+ glue

HOW IT IS MADE

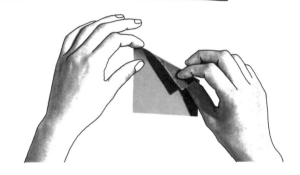

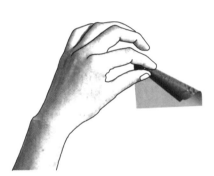

1 Roll the paper into a tube, letting the layers overlap as shown.

2 Glue the loose end of the paper to keep the tube from opening out.

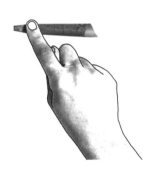

3 Flatten one end a little.

It's done!

What it does

Blow into the Flute-hoot from the flattened end. You should hear a melodious sound. More often than not, the sound you get will seem far from melodious, especially to other people. So what? After all, one person's noise is another person's music.

When it doesn't

Try thinner, stiffer paper and see if it works. If it still doesn't, maybe you aren't blowing the right way. Push the flute a little deeper into your mouth and try again.

Is the flute moist with all that blowing? If it is, it won't hoot, but don't let a damp flute dampen your enthusiasm. Dry it, or make another and keep trying.

Moody Toy?

You might find your flute stubbornly silent sometimes, even if you huff and puff for long. What is wrong? Try remaking the flute: buy different kinds of paper, slightly stiffer and thinner and work with it. This time around you might be lucky. If you are not, take your flute for a walk and see if it works in a different place. Or take it into a quiet room and see if it does better there. Or try to huff and puff a few days later.

Your flute might be a moody flute and work only in certain places and on certain days.

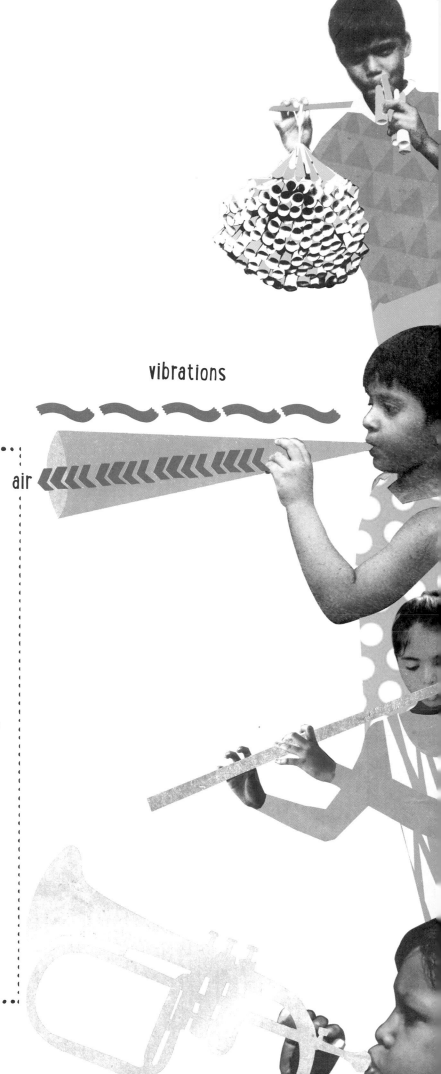

vibrations

air

Vibration

The flute hoots because when you blow into it, air flows through the narrow mouthpiece, and makes the paper vibrate. If the weather is humid, the paper absorbs moisture, and loses elasticity, so it does not vibrate.

→ Try

Use a peepal or banana leaf to make the flute.

Make it with different kinds of paper.
Do all of them work?

Try different lengths and note how the note changes.

Is it possible to get different notes from the same flute?

→ Think

Why should the end of the flute be flattened, before blowing into it? Could it have something to do with the way the air enters the flute when you blow?

Many musical instruments use this principle of vibration that is caused when air escapes through a hole.

How is this flute different from a real one?

Hint: this flute works on the principle of vibration. Real flutes have holes down their length and work on another principle: resonance of air in a column.

Hum

You will need

+ foil or shiny wrapping paper, 12 x 6 cm
+ string, 40 to 50 cm
+ eraser
+ glue
+ scissors

Why does the Hum hum?
Because it's glum?
It can't keep mum?
It's chewing gum?
Perhaps it just likes to hum.

HOW IT IS MADE

1 Tie the eraser to one end of the string.

2 Cut the paper into a semi-circle, about 10 cm in diameter.

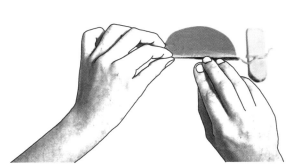

3 Fold the edge and glue it over the string, close to the eraser.

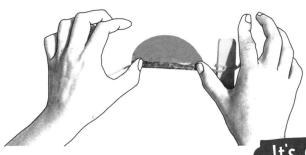

It's done!

22

What it does

Hold the end of the string, and swing the Hum around swiftly, to make it hum. Just be careful not to hit anybody on the head with the eraser.

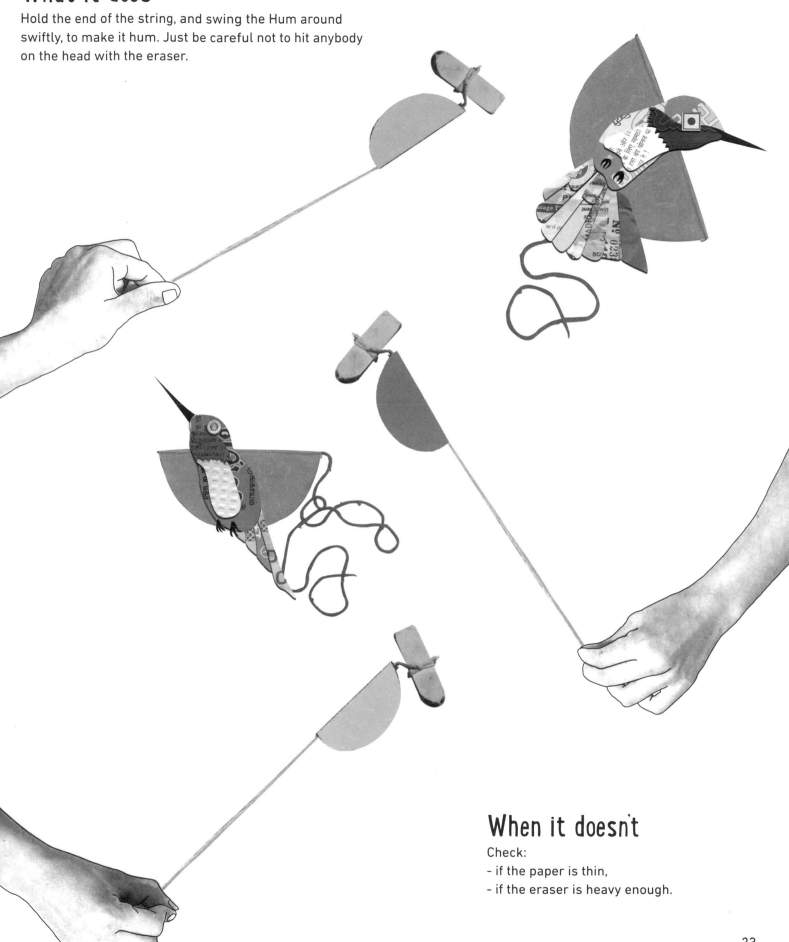

When it doesn't

Check:
- if the paper is thin,
- if the eraser is heavy enough.

Rat-a-tat

You will need

+ a button
+ a bottle cap
+ a rubber band
+ a piece of string
+ scissors

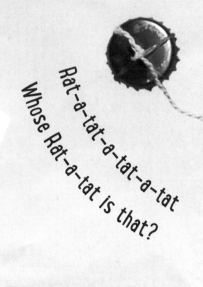

Rat-a-tat-a-tat-a-tat
Whose Rat-a-tat is that?

HOW IT IS MADE

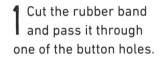

1 Cut the rubber band and pass it through one of the button holes.

2 Tie the rubber band around the bottle cap with the button at the top.

3 Tie a string to the button and make many knots along the length of the string.

It's done!

What it does

Hold the bottle cap in one hand and gently pull
the string with the other, running your fingers over
the knots, from one end to the other. Rat-a-tat-a-tat!
Each one makes a different noise.

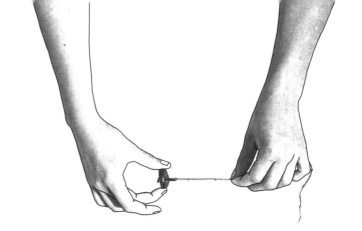

When it doesn't

Are the knots big enough? Are they too far apart or
too close? Don't move your fingers too slow or too fast.
Check if the rubber band is tight.

The Penguin Game

Every Rat-a-tat makes a different noise. Would you be able to recognise
yours from other Rat-a-tats? To ensure that you do so, you might want
to try out this game with some of your friends. It is called 'The Penguin
Game'. Penguins recognise the individual calls of other penguins: of their
mates, babies, parents, friends from amongst the calls of thousands
of other penguins. See if you could likewise recognise the
sound of your Rat-a-tat.

The game starts with each of you making a Rat-a-
tat. When done, imagine that each of the Rat-a-
tats is a baby penguin. The maker of the toy is
the mother penguin. Now one of you gather
all the baby penguins and make them
go 'rat-a-tat', one by one. How many
mothers can recognise their children
by the sound?

What happens if you don't
recognise your baby's sound?
Nothing really—because you
are all not real penguins. If you
were, then your child will have
to wait for his mother for a long
time. And if he is hungry by any
chance, he might starve!

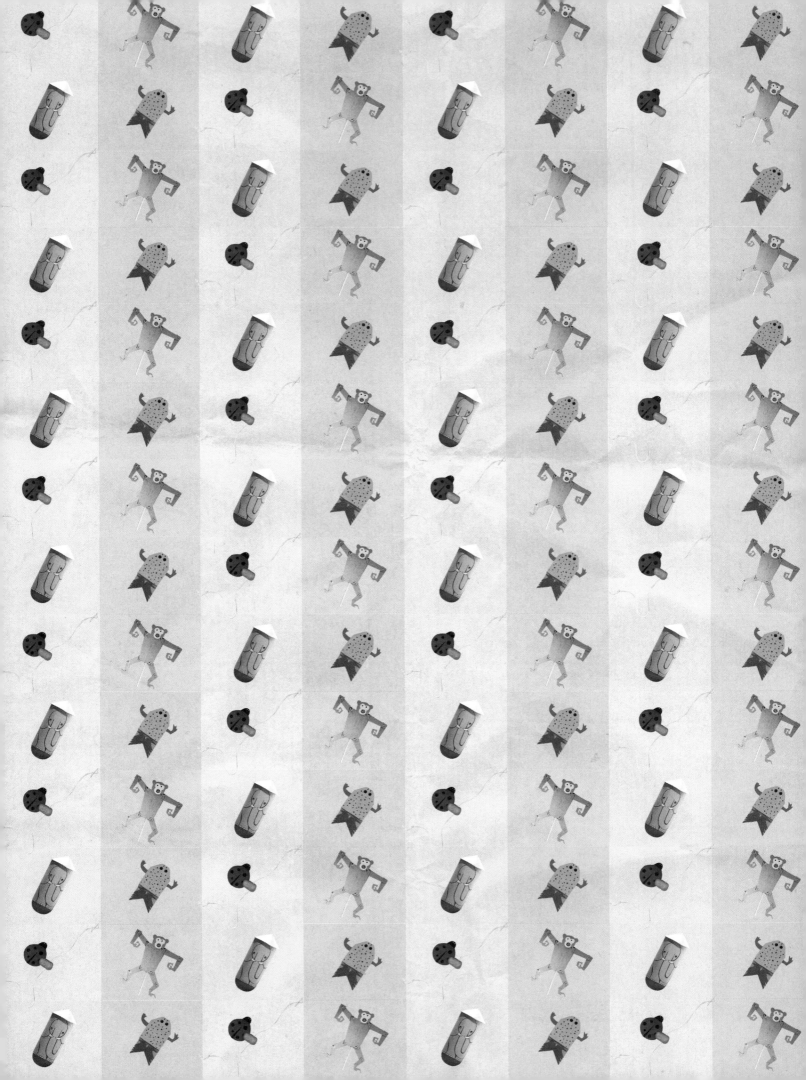

TOYS THAT DANCE

Jitter-bug

page 28

Twist

page 30

Hip-hop

page 33

Rock-n-roll

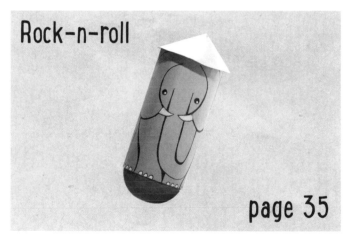

page 35

Jitter-bug

You will need

+ a small lump of clay
+ a piece of string, 50 cm
+ chart paper or thin cardboard
+ scissors
+ glue

The Jitter-bug is an odd sort of critter
It always seems to be in a twitter

Shiver and shake
Quiver and quake

That is the way the Jitter-bugs jitter.

HOW IT IS MADE

1 Make a small bullet out of the clay.

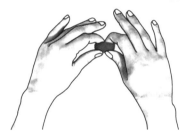

2 Make a hole and a cut as shown. Let it dry.

3 Pass the string through the hole. You could tie a few knots at each end of the string so that the bullet does not slip through it.

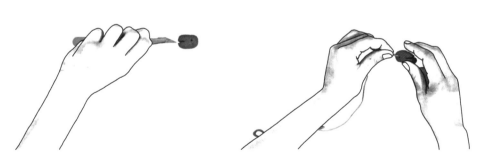

4 Cut out the chart paper in the shape of a bug, or any other shape, and glue it into the cut on the bullet.

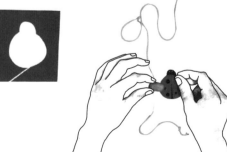

It's done!

What it does

Hold the string vertically and stretch it tight.
The Jitter-bug jitters its way down.

When it doesn't

Check if the hole in the clay bullet is too big.
If it is, the Jitter-bug will slide down quickly.
If it is too small, it will get stuck and won't
be able to move at all.

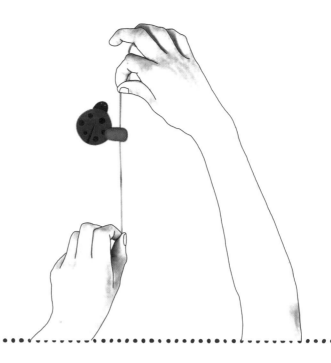

Friction and Elasticity

When you hold the string taut, the clay bullet slips down
a short length of the string. The weight of the bullet acts
on the centre of gravity (CoG) and makes the bullet tilt
downwards (fig. 1). As it tilts, the bullet stops moving
because of the friction acting on the string at the hole.

Now, the string inside the bullet is bent out of shape and
no longer straight. However, the elasticity of the string
causes it to jerk back straight. And, hence, the bullet tilts
upwards (fig. 2). This causes it to move down the string
till gravity causes it to tilt down again. This process is
repeated as the Jitter-bug dances down the length.

→ Try

Use a shuttle cock instead of the clay bullet.
Does this work?

Try using a thick metal wire instead of the string.
What happens?

What if you use a spring in place of the clay bullet?

→ Think

Which of these will jitter? fig. 3 or fig. 4?

Can you think of a way to make the bullet in fig. 4 jitter?

Hint: shift the centre of gravity to one side by adding
weight to it.

If you attach something flat and horizontal to the
clay bullet, the air resistance acts upwards on it and
prevents it from jerking. So it comes down slowly.

Can you think of something that works on the same
principle?

Hint: what would you wish you had with you if you fell
off a plane? A telephone? A book? A parachute?

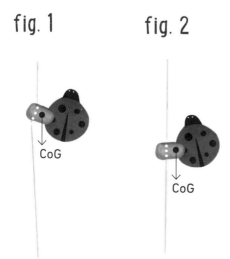

fig. 1   fig. 2

CoG

CoG

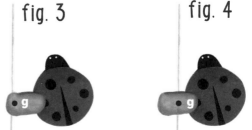

fig. 3   fig. 4

Twist

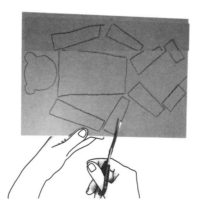

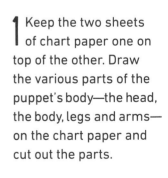

Hold the Twist and turn your wrist
He'll fling his limbs about
Everyone says he has no grace
He dances like a lout.

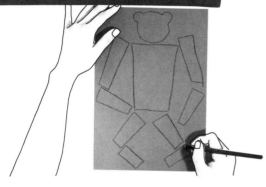

You will need

+ a stick, 25 cm
+ chart paper or packing paper, as needed
+ string, as needed
+ scissors
+ glue

HOW IT IS MADE

1 Keep the two sheets of chart paper one on top of the other. Draw the various parts of the puppet's body—the head, the body, legs and arms—on the chart paper and cut out the parts.

2 Glue the two layers of the head, legs and arms together. Make sure you keep the two layers of the puppet's body apart. You can also add a few extra layers at the limbs to make them heavy.

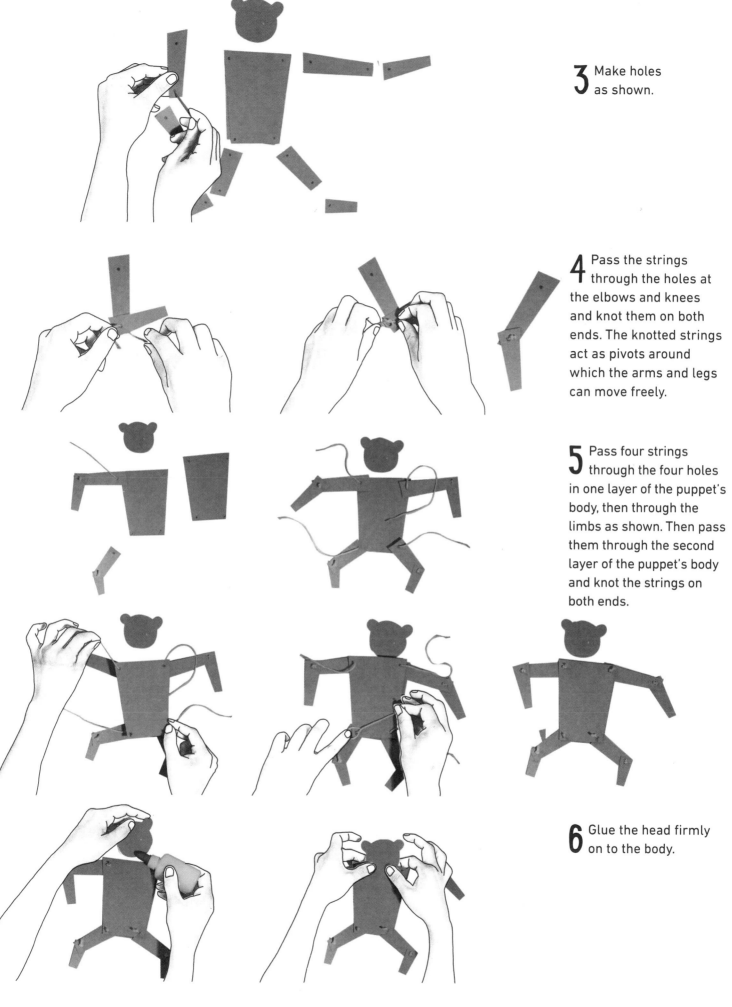

3 Make holes as shown.

4 Pass the strings through the holes at the elbows and knees and knot them on both ends. The knotted strings act as pivots around which the arms and legs can move freely.

5 Pass four strings through the four holes in one layer of the puppet's body, then through the limbs as shown. Then pass them through the second layer of the puppet's body and knot the strings on both ends.

6 Glue the head firmly on to the body.

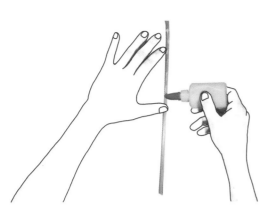

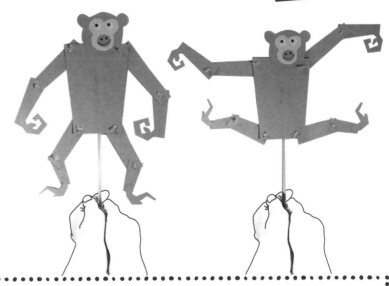

7 Now push the stick between the two layers of the body, then glue the two layers together.

It's done!

What it does

Hold the stick between your palms and twist it with a jerk. The Twist will do a wild jig.

When it doesn't

If the limbs are too tightly tied at the joints, they won't move. They need to be loosely jointed. Also, the ends of limbs should be slightly heavy. If you want the Twist to twist wildly, you can make the limbs really long.

Centrifugal Force

When the stick is twisted, the circular movement creates a centrifugal force. This force acts on the limbs, pulling them outwards. The centrifugal force acting on an object depends upon the mass of the object, and the velocity or speed of the rotation.

→ Try

Twist the stick fast and slow, and see how it affects the movement of the limbs.

Make the limbs longer. Does the Twist become a better dancer or does it make him more loutish?

Hint: centrifugal force is inversely proportional to the radius (r) along which it acts.

→ Think

Can you guess why the Twist dances better if the limbs are heavy at the ends?

Hint: the centrifugal force acting on an object is directly proportional to the mass of the object.

See appendix for more!

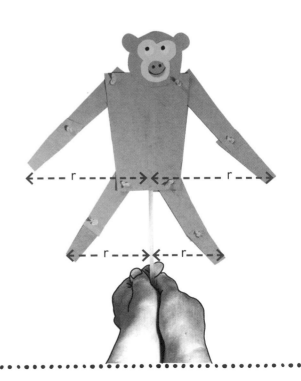

Hip-hop

You will need

+ a piece of card paper 10 x 5 cm
+ colour paper
+ marker
+ scissors

There was a young frog called Flip-flop
He was learning to leap and to hop
But when he went for a race
He couldn't keep pace
So instead he danced the Hip-hop.

HOW IT IS MADE

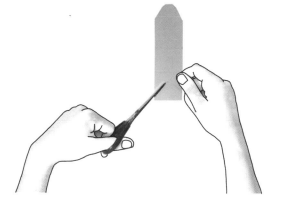

1 Cut the paper as shown.

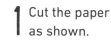

2 Fold one end as shown.

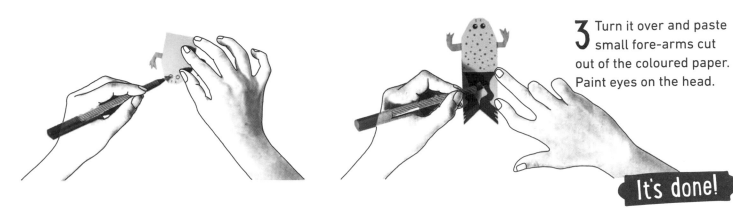

3 Turn it over and paste small fore-arms cut out of the coloured paper. Paint eyes on the head.

What it does

Tap the Hip-hop on its rear end, to make it leap forward.

When it doesn't

The fold at the back has to act like a spring. If you press the folds down too flat, it may not work.

Frog Race

Line up all the Hip-hops. Draw a finishing line. On getting the start signal, all the Hip-hops must leap towards the finishing line.

The Hip-hops that turn turtle are disqualified—no turtles allowed in a Hip-hop race.

Rock-n-roll

You will need

+ a piece of paper, 10 x 20 cm
+ clay
+ scissors
+ glue

Push or shove or biff or bop
Rock-n-roll will never drop.

HOW IT IS MADE

1 Make a small, shallow bowl out of the clay, about 5 cm in diameter and 2 cm high. Let it dry.

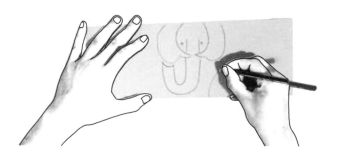

2 Paint a face on the paper. You could also paint something else—a face with a body, or even a geometrical design.

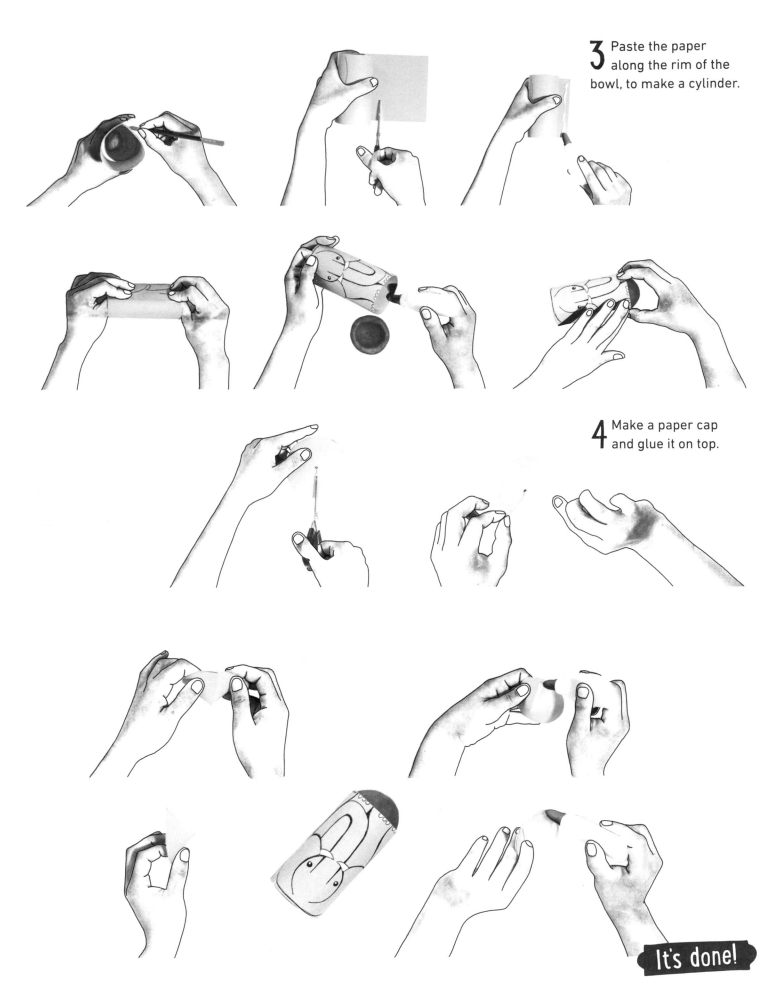

3 Paste the paper along the rim of the bowl, to make a cylinder.

4 Make a paper cap and glue it on top.

It's done!

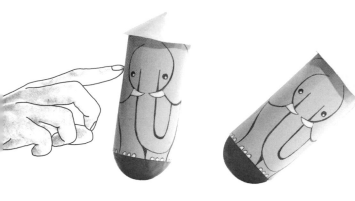

What it does

Give the Rock-n-roll a little push, and it will begin to rock back and forth. Push it hard, and see if you can make it fall.

When it doesn't

Does it fall off to a side instead of rocking? Maybe it is too heavy on top. Or is the paper cylinder too long? Try cutting it shorter. The bowl should be shallow, with a smooth base. If it is deep, it won't be stable and will topple over easily.

Stability and Centre of Gravity

Can you guess why this toy rocks?

When the bowl is in its stable position (fig. 1) the weight of the pot (fg) acts downwards through the centre of gravity (CoG), which is at its lowest point.

According to Newton's third law of motion, when one object applies a force on another, the second object exerts an equal and opposite force of reaction on the first. So the floor exerts an equal and opposite force of reaction (fr) on the bowl at the supporting position (b). The two forces fg and fr act in opposite directions along the same line through the CoG, so the bowl is stable in this position. When the bowl is tilted, the base touches the floor at a new point (b1) (fig. 2). Hence, fr now acts upwards through b1, while fg still pulls downwards through g. These two forces together result in an anti-clockwise movement. When it reaches its stable position, it swings beyond, because of the momentum it has gathered.

→ Try

Make a deep bowl, and try to make it rock. If it is really deep, it will not tilt back. Can you figure out why?

Hint: draw a similar diagram. The CoG will be much higher because of the deep bowl. The point where the base touches the floor (b1) will be towards its left, so the resultant movement will be clockwise.

Make the upper cylinder long and heavy, and give the Rock-n-roll a push. Will it rock?

→ Think

Why does a ball roll?

The centre of gravity of the ball is at its centre. That means, whichever way you turn it, the centre of gravity is always exactly above the point at which it touches the floor.

fig. 1   fig. 2   fig. 3

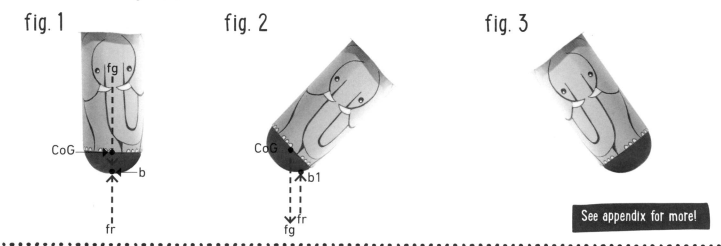

See appendix for more!

TOYS THAT PLAY TRICKS

Clap-trap

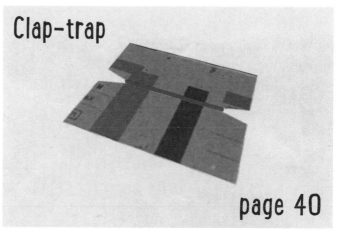

page 40

Flower-power

page 42

Pop-up

page 45

Clap-trap

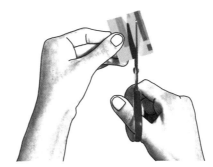

You will need
+ two cardboard pieces, 4 x 5 cm each
+ a rubber band
+ scissors

Find an unsuspecting chap

Trap him with a startling clap.

HOW IT IS MADE

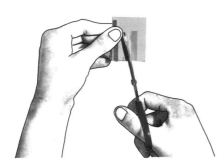

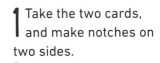

1 Take the two cards, and make notches on two sides.

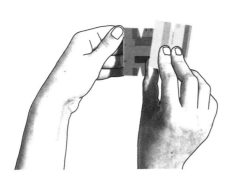

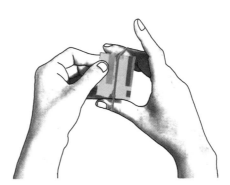

2 Place the two cards together and stretch the rubber band over them, along the notches.

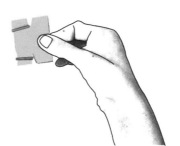

3 Gently open the cards, like a book. See that the rubber band doesn't snap. Fold the cards in the opposite direction and hold them tight. The trap is set to spring.

It's done!

What it does

Throw the Clap-trap into the air. It jumps with a loud clap, making your friends leap in fright.

When it doesn't

If the rubber band is taut enough, and the cardboard is thick enough, it does.

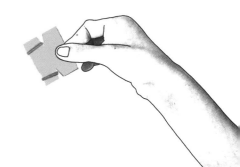

Conversion of Kinetic Energy into Sound

It is quite obvious that the noise is produced because the two pieces of cardboard clap against each other. Once you make the toy, it is also clear that it is the rubber band that causes the clapping. But how?

When the rubber band is stretched, it stores energy. This is called elastic energy. When the Clap-trap is thrown, the elastic energy is converted to kinetic energy. This causes the two cards to leap into the air and flip over to their original position. The kinetic energy is then converted to sound energy, which is why you hear the clap.

→ Try

Make the Clap-trap with a loose rubber band and a tight one. What difference do you notice? Can you explain the difference?

Hint: the greater the tension in the rubber band, the more the elastic energy.

→ Think

In the Clap-trap, stored elastic energy (the tension in the rubber band) is converted to kinetic energy (the leaping book) and sound energy (the clap).

Energy never gets destroyed, so where did it come from in the first place?

Hint: who stretched the rubber band?

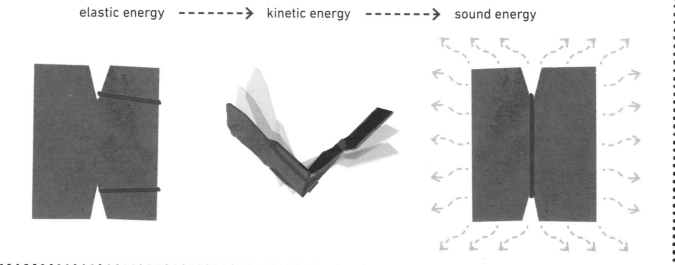

elastic energy - - - - - - -→ kinetic energy - - - - - - -→ sound energy

Flower-power

You will need

+ kite paper, 7 x 25 cm
+ coloured paper
+ 2 cardboard pieces, 8 x 10 cm each
+ glue
+ scissors

It comes and goes
This mystery flower
Does it have some
Magic power?

HOW IT IS MADE

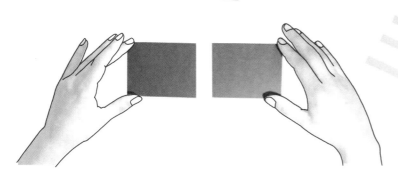

1 Keep the two cards side by side along the shorter side. Cut 3 strips of 15 x 1.5 cm from the coloured paper.

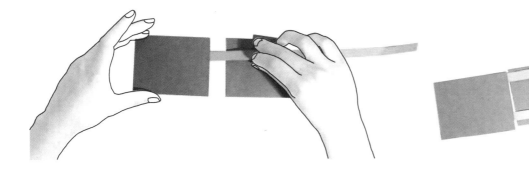

2 Place two strips about 3 cm apart on the first card, with the ends going under the second card.

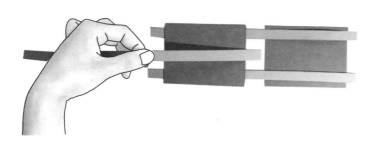

3 Place one strip on the second card, with the end going under the first.

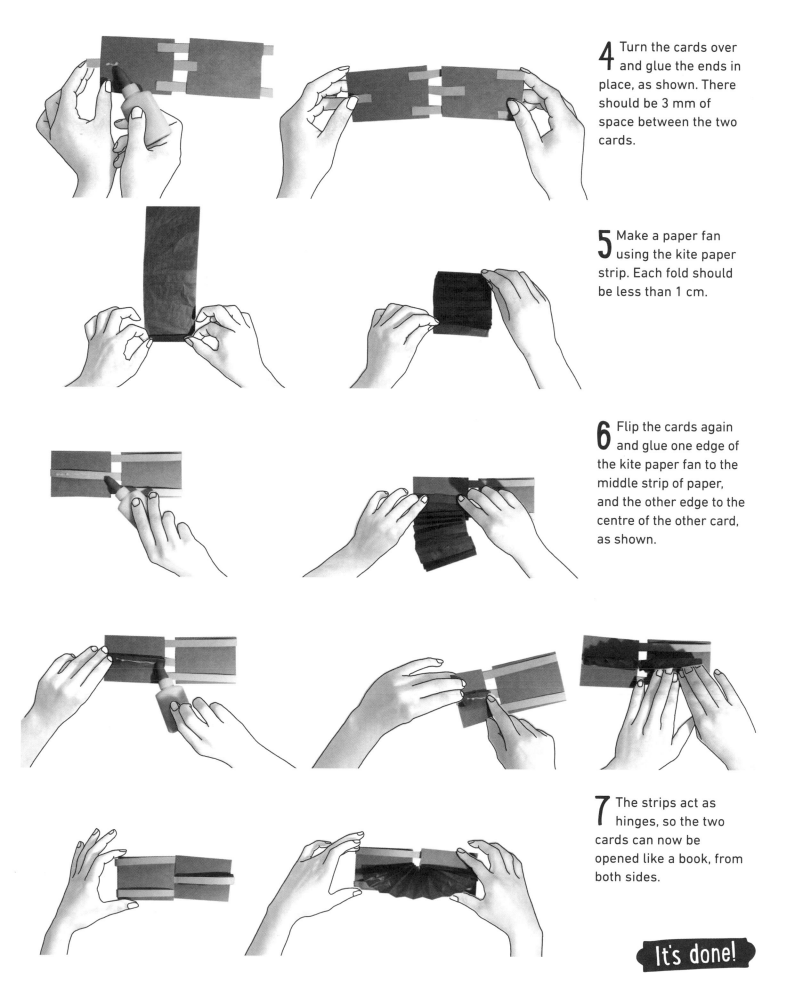

4 Turn the cards over and glue the ends in place, as shown. There should be 3 mm of space between the two cards.

5 Make a paper fan using the kite paper strip. Each fold should be less than 1 cm.

6 Flip the cards again and glue one edge of the kite paper fan to the middle strip of paper, and the other edge to the centre of the other card, as shown.

7 The strips act as hinges, so the two cards can now be opened like a book, from both sides.

It's done!

What it does

Hold one card and release the other card, letting it fall open. Take care to show the side where the flower is hidden. Then holding the lower card, quickly let the upper card fall back, and flip it downwards: Flower-power!

When it doesn't

Check if the hinges are fixed the right way. If they are okay, there is only thing that can go wrong: the flower that is supposed to be hidden is quickly spotted by the audience. This would ruin the show, so make the fan narrow, and use thin paper that will not bulge.

You need to be quick and cunning. Distract the audience by talking and waving your arms about. It would also help to seat the audience at a distance.

Magic Show

You can gross out your friends with this magic show. Cut out the cardboard pieces in the shape of an apple, and instead of a flower, put in a folded strip of paper which looks like a worm.

First open the apple on the good side, where the worm cannot be seen, and show it to your audience.

You: Isn't it a nice apple?

Audience: Yes! Yes!

You: Would you like to eat it?

Audience: Yes! Yes!

When their mouths have started watering, flip over the apple. Out pops the worm.

Audience: Aaarghh!

Variations on Flower-power?

Worm in a garden

Smiling/frowning face

Flowers on both sides

Family tree

Storyboard: a different story on each side

Pop-up

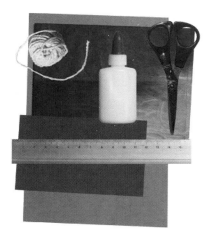

You will need

+ two A4 sheets or two sheets from a glossy magazine, 20 cm and 9 cm long
+ kite paper
+ string
+ scissors
+ glue

Needs no prop-up
Just some chop-up
Glue-up, mop-up
It'll crop-up
With no flop-up.

HOW IT IS MADE

Tube A

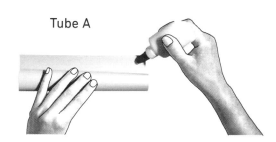

Tube B

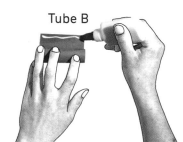

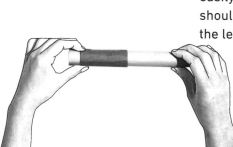

1 Make two tubes, Tube A and Tube B as shown. Roll Tube A with the 20 cm long paper, using a pencil to support paper rolling, so that the diameter is about 1.5 cm. Now roll Tube B with the 9 cm long paper, such that it can slide over Tube A easily. Length of Tube B should be less than half of the length of Tube A.

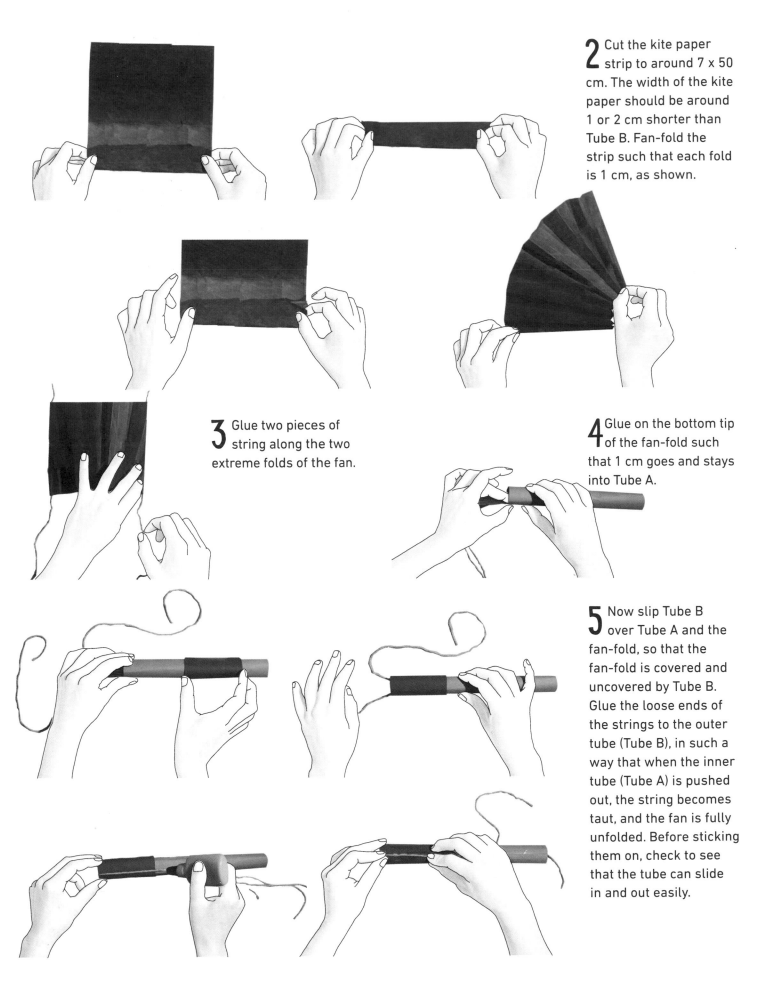

2 Cut the kite paper strip to around 7 x 50 cm. The width of the kite paper should be around 1 or 2 cm shorter than Tube B. Fan-fold the strip such that each fold is 1 cm, as shown.

3 Glue two pieces of string along the two extreme folds of the fan.

4 Glue on the bottom tip of the fan-fold such that 1 cm goes and stays into Tube A.

5 Now slip Tube B over Tube A and the fan-fold, so that the fan-fold is covered and uncovered by Tube B. Glue the loose ends of the strings to the outer tube (Tube B), in such a way that when the inner tube (Tube A) is pushed out, the string becomes taut, and the fan is fully unfolded. Before sticking them on, check to see that the tube can slide in and out easily.

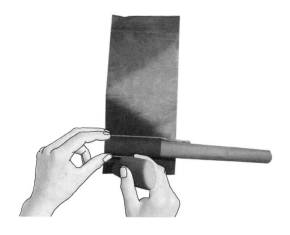

What it does

Show the tube to your friends. Ask them what it is: a pen? a trumpet? Then mutter something and swish your arms around to distract them, and when they are not watching, push the inner tube out from below. The fan pops up, amazing the open-mouthed audience.

When it doesn't

If the fan is too thick, it might get stuck in the tube. Either the tube should be widened, or the fan should be made thinner. It is always best to practise before you gather an audience, or your Pop-up might be a flop-up.

It's done!

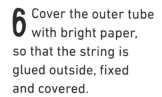

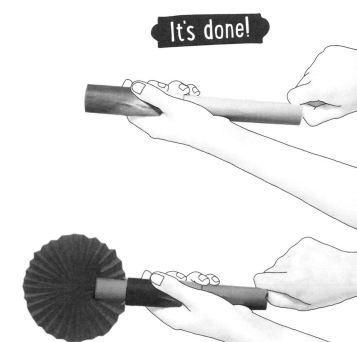

FOLDING & UNFOLDING

The object that pops up has two basic attributes:

1. It can be folded so that it fits into the tube.

2. When it pops out, it can open up fully. The string attached to the fan pulls the ends downwards, and the fan opens out.

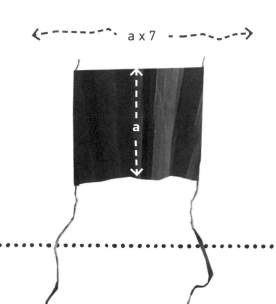

$a \times 7$

a

→ Try

Can you think of something other than a fan that can be used as a Pop-up?

→ Think

While making the fan, the length of the paper should be about seven times the width. Can you figure out why?

Hint: the perimeter of the fan is $2\pi r$, where r is the width (radius) of the fan. $\pi = 3.14$ (approx.)

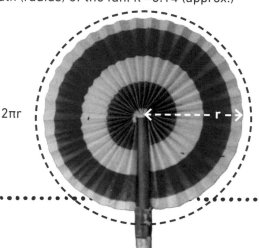

$2\pi r$

r

TOYS THAT MOVE
WITH THE WIND

Retpocileh

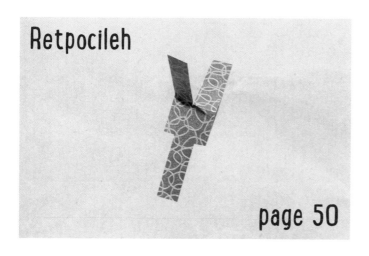

page 50

Flutter-fly

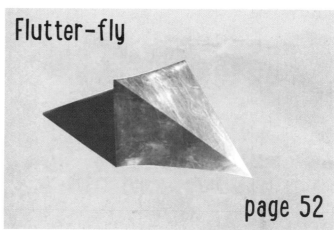

page 52

Spinning Sardine

page 54

Naf

page 56

Retpocileh

Is it a sparrow?

Is it a jay?

No, no, no, it's Retpocileh.

You will need
+ a strip of paper, 8 x 2 cm
+ scissors

HOW IT IS MADE

1 Cut one long slit down half the length of the strip, and two small vertical slits on two sides about 1 cm above the horizontal slit.

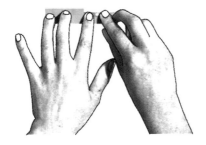 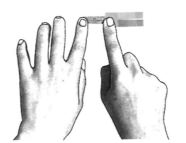

2 Fold the paper inwards on both sides, at the vertical slits, as shown.

3 Fold the upper part out on opposite sides, as shown. These are the blades.

It's done!

Try making Retpocilehs with as many types of paper as possible, and in different sizes. Get them to spin from different heights.

You could also look around in your garden or playground for other things which spin like Retpocilehs. You would be surprised to find that some flowers and seeds spin exactly like they do—oleander flowers, for instance. There may be others as well.

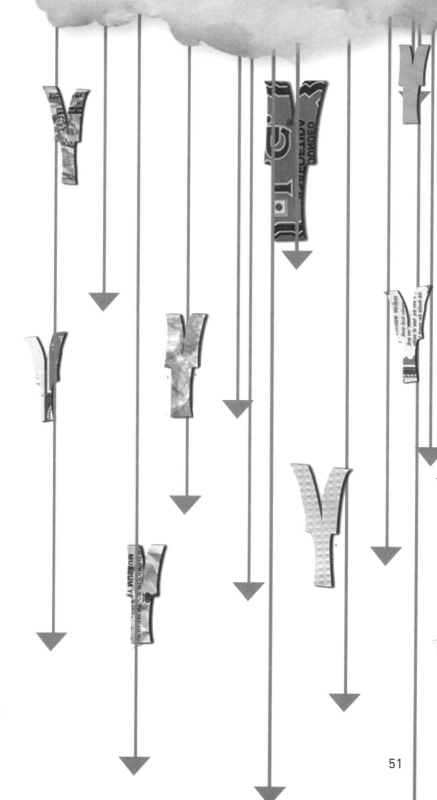

What it does

Fling your Retpocileh from a height and watch it twirl and descend. You can also accompany it with strange sounds if you like. Or else watch it silently.

When it doesn't

If your Retpocileh doesn't rotate, try changing the length of the blades and of the base.

51

Flutter-fly

You will need
+ a square piece of paper, 10 x 10 cm
+ scissors
+ ruler

Blow blow blow your breath
Without a word or mutter
Merrily merrily merrily merrily
Flutter-fly will flutter.

HOW IT IS MADE

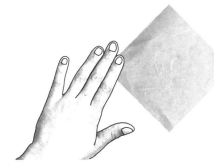

1 Fold the paper along the diagonal to make a crease.

2 Decorate your Flutter-fly. Or you can cut it into a different shape. Make sure it is symmetrical: when you fold it at the centre, the two sides should overlap exactly.

It's done!

What it does
Place the Flutter-fly on the floor or on a table. The central creased part should be slightly raised. Now blow at it along the surface on which it is kept. It flutters and moves.

When it doesn't
First make sure the fold is alright. If you blow at the top of the Flutter-fly, it may not flutter. Keep blowing from different angles until you get it right.

Air Pressure and Lift

A good way to think about this toy is to think about how airplanes fly. Airplanes fly because of the curved shape of the wings where the air pressure underneath it is higher than that of the pressure above. This difference in pressure is caused by the curve of the wing where some of the air is pushed upwards causing a drop in pressure and some of the air is pushed down causing a rise in pressure. The difference in pressure causes a resultant upward force, or lift.

The pressure is not uniform over the surface. The point at which the lift acts (CoL) is called the centre of lift (fig. 2). For an object to be balanced, the centre of lift and centre of gravity must lie on the same line. But does all this explain why the Flutter-fly flutters? Only partly. When you blow at the Flutter-fly, the resultant lift makes it rise (fig. 3), but the lift is not enough to counter its weight, so it comes down again. The Flutter-fly has a crease along the diagonal, so the toy is balanced at two corners. When you blow at it, the lift causes it to tilt. As you keep blowing, the wind pushes the far side up again. This process is repeated continuously, so the Flutter-fly tilts backwards and forwards rapidly.

→ Try

Make a Flutter-fly in the shape of an arrow-head. Now blow at the tip. It flutters. When you blow from the other side, it almost takes off. The lift is obviously greater. So the amount of lift depends on the shape in relation to the direction of the air flow.

→ Think

Some school textbooks have this to say about pressure change: it happens because the air on the curved upper surface of the wing has further to travel than that below the flat underneath surface, meaning it must travel faster to arrive at the other side of the wing at the same time. But can this theory explain how several airplanes sometimes fly upside down?

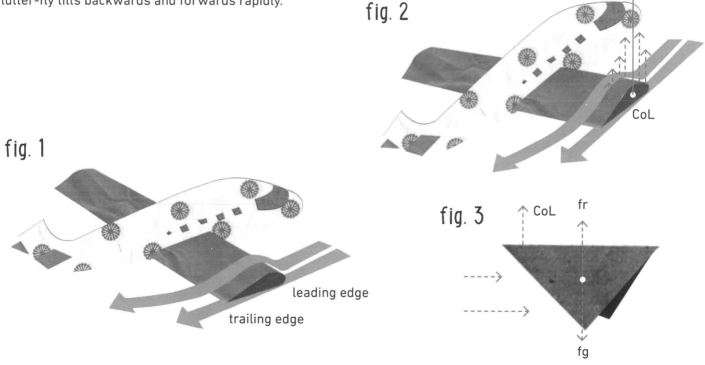

fig. 1

leading edge

trailing edge

fig. 2

CoL

fig. 3

↑ CoL   fr

fg

Spinning Sardine

Watch the sardines
Flying and spinning
The last one to land
Is the one that's winning.

You will need
+ a strip of paper, 1.2 x 15 cm
+ scissors
+ ruler

HOW IT IS MADE

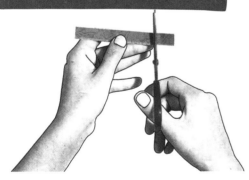

1 Make two slits on the piece of paper, as shown.

2 Fold the paper at the centre and lock the slits into each other.

It's done!

What it does

Throw the Sardine into the air. It flies down, spinning round and round.

When it doesn't

If the strip is too broad, it may not spin well. Try making the strip narrower. Maybe the 'tail' of the sardine is too short or too long.

Turning Force: Horizontal Axis

This toy works in the same way as the Retpocileh. The difference is that since the most stable position of the Sardine is horizontal, it spins horizontally rather than vertically. The two blades that form the tail of the Sardine are bent at opposite angles with respect to the horizontal axis.

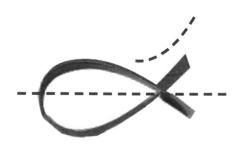

→ Try

Make a broad Sardine and a narrow one, and launch them together from the same height. Which one spins better? Which one lands first?

→ Think

Suppose the tail-blades of the Sardine are not bent. What will happen then? Do you think it will rotate?

Naf

You will need

+ 3 strips of paper, 25 x 2.5 cm each
+ pencil
+ scissors
+ ruler

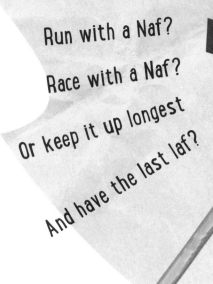

Run with a Naf?

Race with a Naf?

Or keep it up longest

And have the last laf?

HOW IT IS MADE

1 Take the three strips of paper, and fold each of them in half.

2 Interlock them exactly as shown. The open end of each strip is held between the folds of another strip. Pull the ends gently, one by one, till they form a conical shape in the centre.

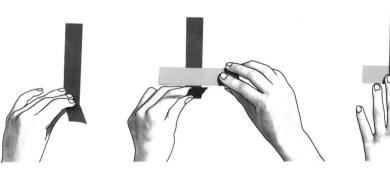

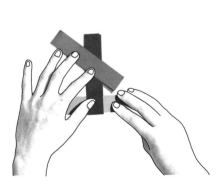

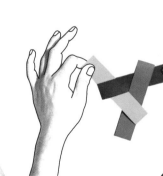

It's done!

What it does

Place one end of a blunt pencil at the centre of the Naf and run with it. It spins round and round. If you drop it from a height, it will spin down.

When it doesn't

Run faster. Or use a different kind of paper.

Naf-a-thon

Race to the finishing line without dropping the Naf.

If you lost, so what? He who reaches last Nafs longest.

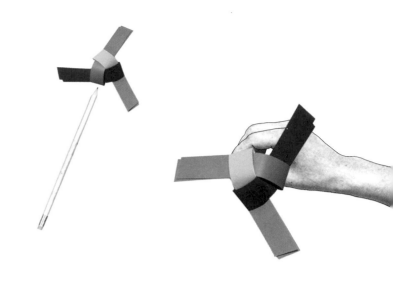

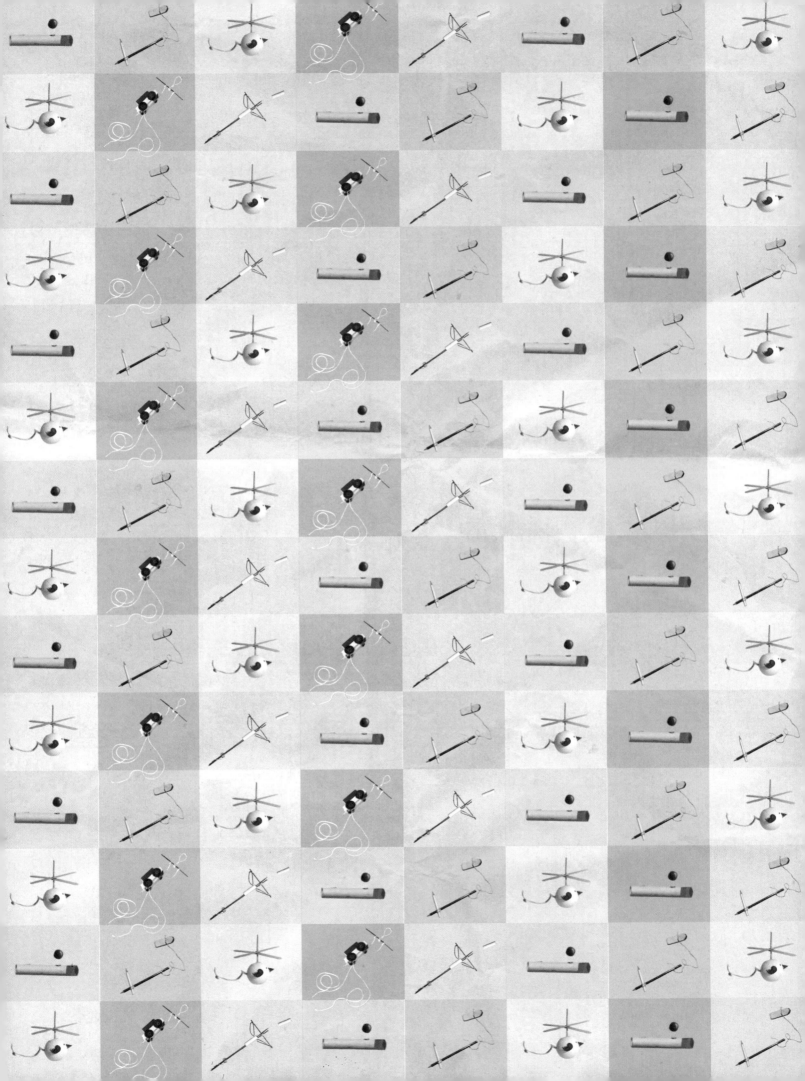

TOYS THAT NEED SKILL

Huff-n-puff

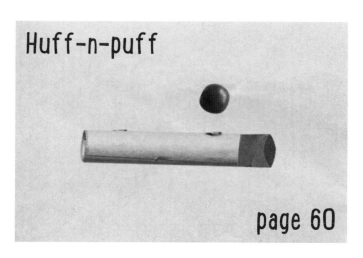

page 60

Pencycle

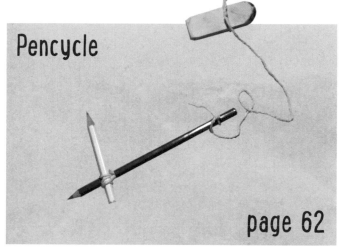

page 62

Yankee

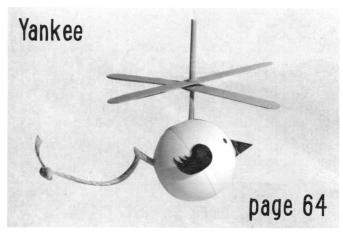

page 64

Creep-jeep

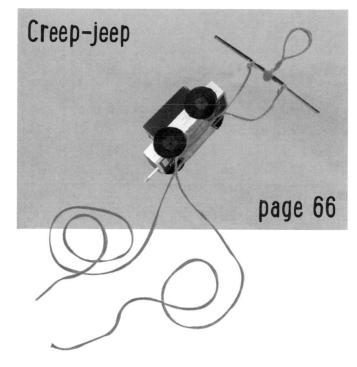

page 66

Shoot-a-reel

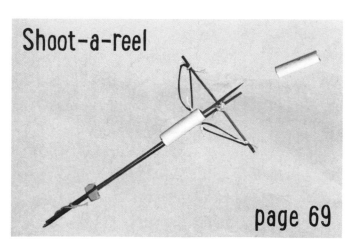

page 69

Huff-n-puff

Huff and puff

The bead goes uff.

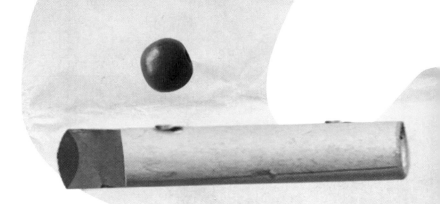

You will need

+ a light bead
+ an empty thread reel
+ chart paper or thin cardboard
+ paper
+ glue

HOW IT IS MADE

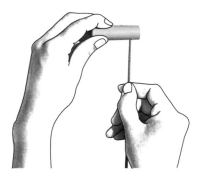

1 Make a small hole in one side of the reel.

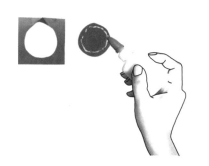

2 Seal off one end of the reel by pasting paper on it.

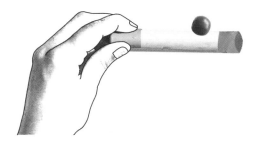

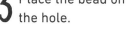

What it does

Blow hard and steadily through the open end of the tube. The bead stays up in the air, spinning.

When it doesn't

If the bead is too heavy or not spherical, it will be difficult to lift and keep it in the air. But if it is a light, round plastic bead, all you need to do is huff and puff till you blow the bead up. Keep trying till you get it.

Air Pressure and Smooth Air-Flow

The air that you blow is channelled through the hole, and exerts a pressure upwards on the bead. This force counters the gravitational force and keeps the bead up. The smooth air-flow around the bead keeps it above the hole. This smooth flow is called laminar flow or streamline flow.

→ Try

Do it with your eyes closed and see what happens.

What happens if you blow too hard?

→ Think

If you use a heavy ball instead of a light one, can you keep it up in the air? Why not?

Hint: you might be able to do it if you have unusually powerful lungs.

61

Pencycle

Keep it going! Don't let it stop!
Keep it spinning! Don't let it drop!

You will need

+ a piece of strong string, 15 cm
+ a long pencil
+ a short pencil
+ an eraser

HOW IT IS MADE

1 Tie the two pencils together, at less than 90 degrees to each other.

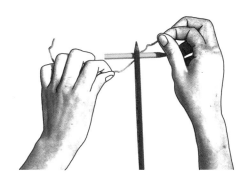

2 Tie the eraser at one end of the piece of string.

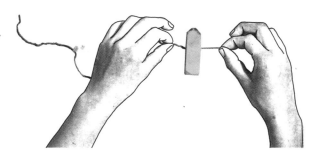

3 Make a groove near the base of the long pencil.

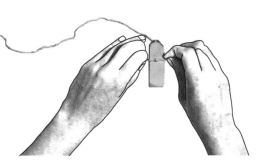

4 Tie the free end of the string along the groove.

It's done!

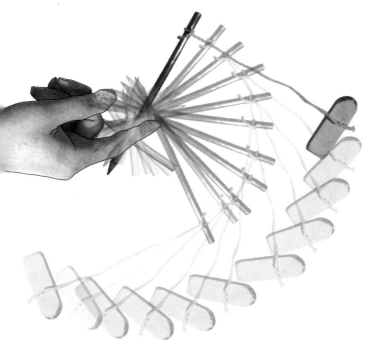

What it does

Place your finger at the angle between the two pencils and twirl the Pencycle around.

When it doesn't

This is like learning to ride a bicycle. At first it looks impossible, then suddenly you get the perfect balance, and you can never unlearn it.

Centrifugal and Centripetal Forces

When the Pencycle rotates, there is a centrifugal force, which pulls the eraser away from your finger, and a centripetal force which pulls it towards your finger. Your finger acts as a pivot (p). You have to shift its position constantly in order to maintain the tension in the string.

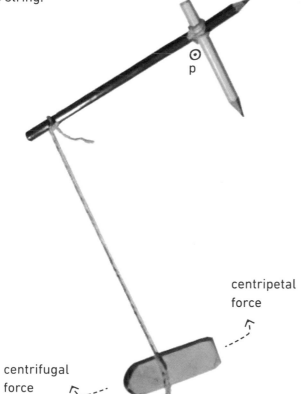

centripetal force

centrifugal force

→ Try

Instead of using two pencils, see if you can find an L-shaped twig.

Try making the toy with different lengths of the string. Why is it difficult to rotate the Pencycle if the string is too long?

Hint: centrifugal force is inversely proportional to the radius of rotation. The longer the string, the greater the radius of rotation.

Instead of the eraser, use a flower. Does it work? Try attaching two flowers, then three, then four ... until you reach a point when the toy does not work.

→ Think

Can you guess why the Pencycle falls off if you slow down the rotation?

Why do you need a certain amount of skill to play with the Pencycle? You have to make sure that at every moment your finger is in contact with both the pencils. Since one side of the angle is open, it requires some dexterity to do this.

Why is it that if the object at the end of the string is too heavy, the Pencycle flies off the finger?

See appendix for more!

Yankee

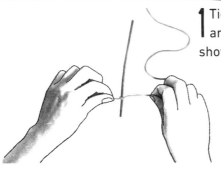

You will need

+ strong string, 30 cm
+ an old table-tennis ball
+ cardboard or ice-cream sticks
+ a stick, 7 cm long, 0.5 cm thick
+ a match

Yankee-panky
Small and spank-y.

HOW IT IS MADE

1 Tie a piece of string around the stick, as shown.

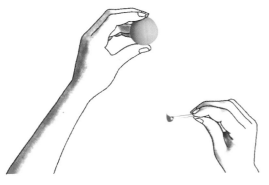

2 Cut out two small strips of cardboard and make a hole at the centre of each of them. You could also use two ice-cream sticks instead.

3 Fix the two pieces cross-wise, onto the other end of the stick.

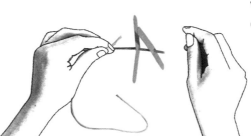

4 Make a hole in the table-tennis ball. An easy way to do this: light a matchstick, blow it out and at once push the burnt end into the ball. The ball is made of plastic, so it melts at that point.

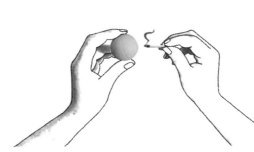

5 Push in the end of the stick with a string around it into the hole.

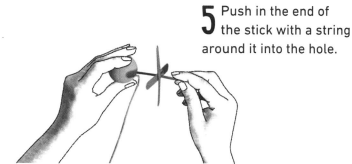

6 Make another hole, at right angles to the first one.

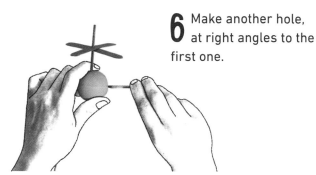

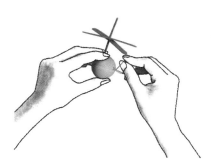

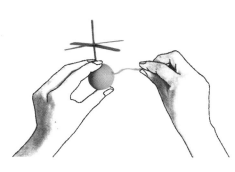

7 Pull out the string through this hole using a pin or wire.

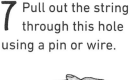

It's done!

What it does

Rotate the cardboard fan round and round until the string is completely wound around the stick. Leave a small bit of string hanging out of the hole. Pull the string with a jerk and release it. The fan on top spins round one way, and then immediately spins the other way, rewinding the string around the stick.

When it doesn't

The trick is in the way you yank the string. You need to pull it with a jerk, but when the string is fully unwound, you have to release it slowly, so that it can rewind itself around the stick. Keep trying. After a while you will be able to spin it continuously.

The Mystery of the Missing Pulp

This toy was originally made in Kerala with a rubber seed. But how did people hollow it out without cracking it?

Toymakers used to make two holes in several rubber seeds and leave them out in the fields, near an anthill. After some time, they would pick up the seeds—which were all nicely hollowed.

Whodunnit? Ants got into the seeds and ate all the pulp in them! See if there are other seeds that get hollowed out by ants.

Creep-jeep

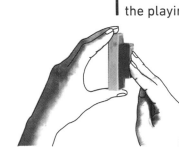

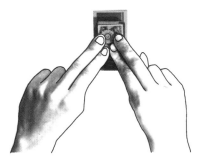

Climbers creepers
Losers? Jeepers!

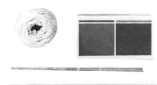

You will need

+ a plastic straw
+ a small stick, 10 cm
+ 2 pieces of string, 60 cm each
+ cardboard, as needed
+ a playing cards box
+ an empty match box
+ glue
+ scissors

HOW IT IS MADE

1 Glue the match box on the playing cards box.

2 Make wheels out of the cardboard and glue them to the sides of the playing cards box.

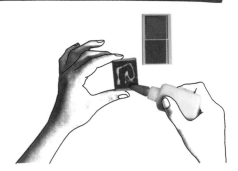

3 Cut three notches on the stick.

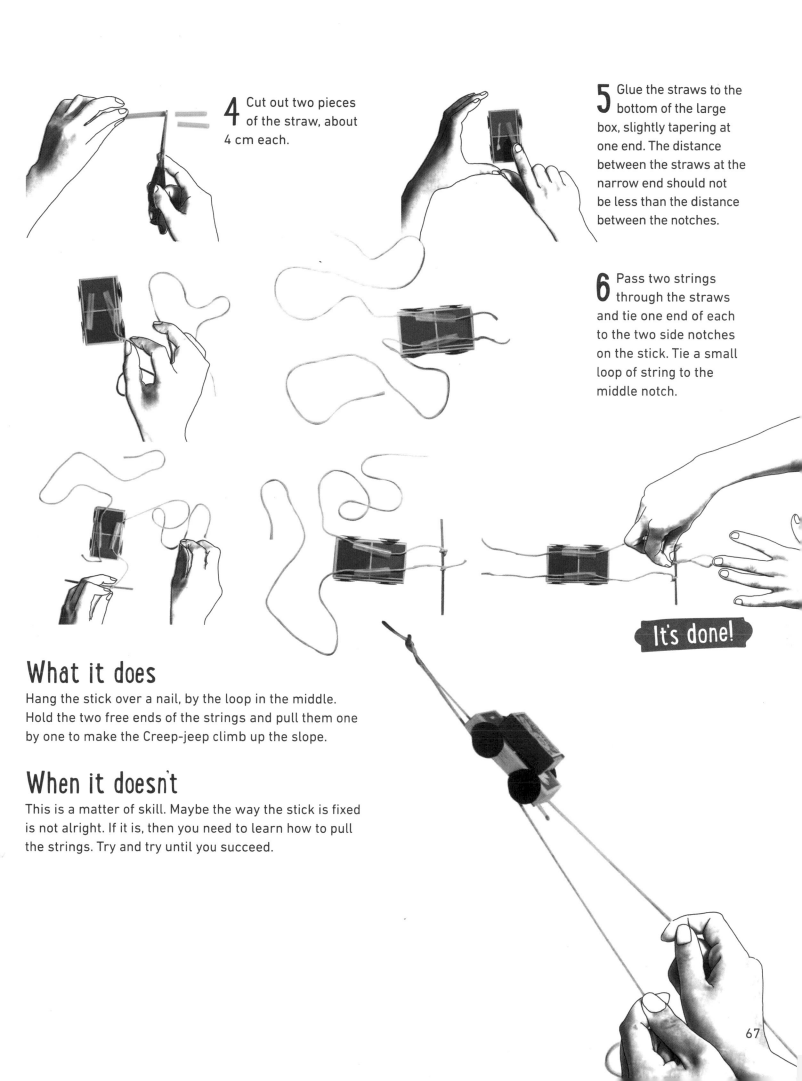

4 Cut out two pieces of the straw, about 4 cm each.

5 Glue the straws to the bottom of the large box, slightly tapering at one end. The distance between the straws at the narrow end should not be less than the distance between the notches.

6 Pass two strings through the straws and tie one end of each to the two side notches on the stick. Tie a small loop of string to the middle notch.

It's done!

What it does

Hang the stick over a nail, by the loop in the middle. Hold the two free ends of the strings and pull them one by one to make the Creep-jeep climb up the slope.

When it doesn't

This is a matter of skill. Maybe the way the stick is fixed is not alright. If it is, then you need to learn how to pull the strings. Try and try until you succeed.

Friction

At the start, the left and right straws are at a and b respectively.

When you pull the right string, the left side of the stick moves upwards. Because of the angle of the straws, the friction causes the string to get jammed in the left straw at a. The right string moves downwards, so the right straw now moves up along the string to a new position c. When you pull the left string, the right straw gets jammed at c. The left string moves downwards, so the left straw moves upwards to d. You get a resultant movement upwards, along the string.

→ Try

Turn the box around so that the straws are tapering downwards. You will find that the Creep-jeep creeps downhill. Observe it carefully and you will see that the same process is at work, but in reverse.

→ Think

What will happen if the straws are perfectly parallel and not tapering towards one end?

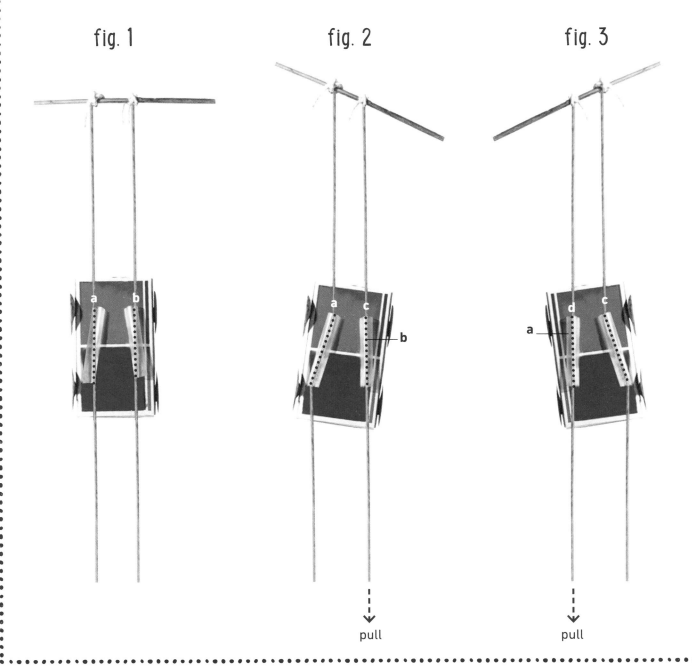

fig. 1

fig. 2

fig. 3

pull

pull

Shoot-a-reel

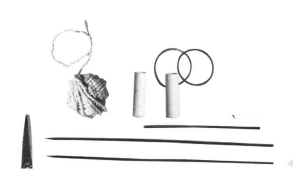

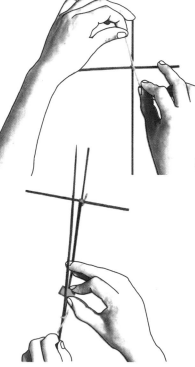

You will need

+ 2 empty thread reels
+ 1 stick, 15 cm
+ 2 sticks, 30 cm each
+ 2 long rubber bands
+ string, as needed
+ scissors

Take your aim
And Shoot-a-reel
If you miss
It's no big deal.

HOW IT IS MADE

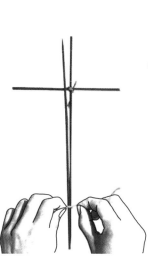

1 Tie the short stick to one of the long sticks, forming a cross.

2 Tie the other long stick to the cross, at the bottom. Wedge an eraser between the two, so that there is a gap of about 2 cm between them at the top.

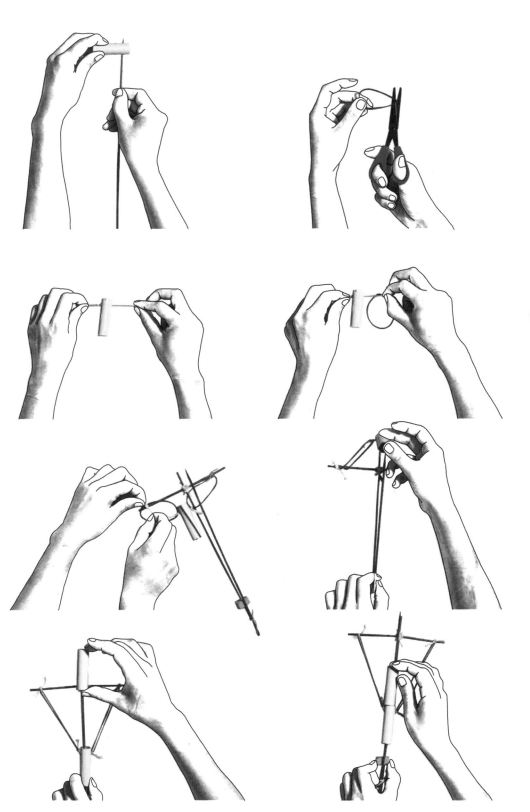

3 Make two holes near the top of one of the thread reels. Cut one rubber band and push it through the holes. Tie the other two rubber bands to the two ends of the cut rubber band.

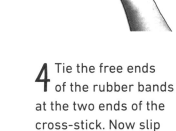

4 Tie the free ends of the rubber bands at the two ends of the cross-stick. Now slip the reel onto the other long stick.

5 Slip the second reel over the first one.

It's done!

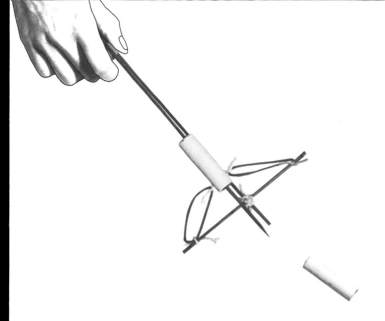

What it does

Pull down the lower reel, stretching the rubber band. Release it suddenly. The upper reel shoots out like an arrow.

When it doesn't

This is a matter of skill. Maybe the way the stick is fixed is not alright. If it is, then you need to learn how to pull the strings.

Energy Conversion

When you pull the fixed reel, elastic energy is stored in the stretched rubber band. When you release it, this elastic energy gets converted to kinetic energy, and the reels move upwards. The free reel shoots out of the Shoot-a-reel.

Try

You can make many kinds of shooting instruments, using this principle. Bow and arrow and catapult are two examples.

Think

What should you do to make your Shoot-a-reel shoot farther?

Hint: increase the elastic energy.

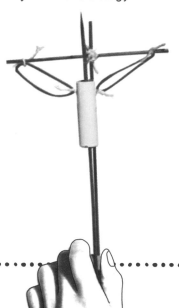

elastic energy  - → kinetic energy

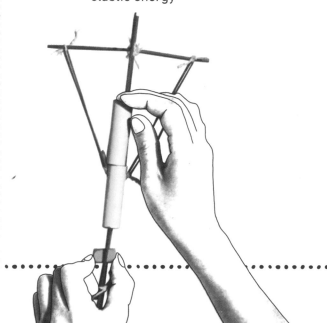

About Play

Reflections on toys and play for parents and educators

There is a free, unscripted and creative aspect to play that is indefinable, and this is a quality that has little to do with expensive toys. Throughout history, children have always played with sticks, pebbles, ropes and wheels—things picked up and turned into toys. These are what we could call 'toys without form', which can stand in for anything, depending on the script or the game. No one but the players can decide what the objects are or will become. Play comes first, toys follow.

Then there are the 'classical' toys that generations of children have played with: dolls, small carts or vehicles, animals made of stuffed cloth… They foster a different kind of play, allowing children to experiment with actions, relationships and feelings that mirror the real, or the longed-for.

Yet another kind of play came into being sometime in the 1960s, when the production of toys and games started on an industrial scale in the West. It did not have too much of an impact on countries such as India until the late 1980s, but we have since 'caught up', and, meanwhile, the toy business has grown into a huge world-wide industry. Apart from some of the classical toys that continue to be made, one of the main thrusts of the toy industry has been the development of playthings which feature well-developed characters that have ready-made friends, settings and stories around them, all created by professionals. Television and other promotional tie-ins extend and reinforce the characters and storylines, so playing with these toys and dolls tends to be within a pre-determined context. These kinds of playthings, which also call for innumerable accessories, are very popular, so in the process of desiring, acquiring and collecting them, the child is turned into a consumer, and a very vulnerable one at that.

The truth is that despite all the marketing claims that are made on their behalf, when the frame of reference around a toy is defined, it actually tends to channel the child's imagination into particular patterns, rather than open it up. It also contributes to children buying into the dreams and values of those who control the market. Clearly, the buying of vast numbers of accessories serves the needs of the industry more than that of the child.

Practically speaking, it's hard to forbid children from playing with such toys. We can only ensure that they also get to play in far more unstructured and improvised ways. But ironically enough, what we would call freewheeling play (which is not tied to commercial products) is more available to poorer children, who ostensibly can't afford anything 'better'.

Affluent children's lives today are also dominated by another factor: the ascendancy of the screen. Virtual play is beginning to overshadow material toys. There are a bewildering number of games and apps in the market, and the number keeps growing. While some of them are certainly quite well-thoughtout, there is one thing they all lack: the sensory and tactile experience that physical material provides. It is this simple earthy physicality that is sadly lacking in most contemporary children's lives, in spite of all the resources available to them. Ironically, yet again, well-to-do children are even more deprived in this sense.

So what can we do, as concerned adults? We certainly cannot turn the clock back, wish away developments, or censor children all the time. What we can do is to be vigilant when we make choices, and not accept everything that the toy industry exhorts children to possess. We can also create opportunities for children to experience other kinds of play, with very different sorts of playthings, some of which children

and adults can make together—like the toys in this book. Parents or educators with pre-teen children will find that such intervention is both possible and productive. At this stage, children still look up to and are influenced by the adults who care for them, and we hope this book will create a context for this kind of mediation.

The process of making these toys will engage the child with materiality. She will need to handle different materials, experiment with them and get to know their properties, while working through the challenge of making sure the plaything 'works' in the way it is meant to. Once a toy is ready, there is a very special quality to the play it enables. This is mediated by the creative relationship that a child has to something she has made herself—this creates a context for very different kinds of play.

These are things we noticed ourselves, when we made these toys with a group of children in a toy-making workshop (on which this book is based). The children in our workshop were between 9 and 12 years of age. It was a mixed group, with kids from middle-class as well as working-class schools. We saw that when children (from both kinds of schools) are actively absorbed in making their own toys, they seem far more open to all kinds of possibilities, and less prone to pass quick judgment. They are in unknown territory. We also noticed that older children who wandered into the workshop were equally curious. Their interest was essentially provoked by how and why the toys worked, so we asked them to join in as well. (Their inputs form the basis of the science sections of this book.)

The workshop gave us several interesting insights on the role of toys and play in children's lives. The toys we made together turned out to be rich points of departure to think and talk about a number of issues, from science, history to consumerism, gender, and much more.

So here are some of our reflections, which we have worked into themes for adults to think through: each topic is loosely tied to the process of making a particular toy. The points we make are suggestive and wide-ranging, rather than prescriptive. Each theme is also offset by illustrations that are playfully excursive. Together, we'd like the words and images to prompt parents and educators to explore these concerns in a radically fresh light.

What are folk toys?

The toys featured in this book are based on so-called folk toys, playthings that were made and sold by small-time artisans all over India. They used inexpensive local materials to come up with an unbelievable variety of charming and affordable toys. Individual artisans, families and craft communities would travel around selling their wares in villages and towns. They also 'mass produced' them for fairs and festivals. Today, such fairs are full of stalls selling cheap plastic toys, numbing in their lack of variety and imagination.

Folk toymakers were amazingly innovative, creating playthings with whatever material was readily available, often substituting other material when they didn't find what they needed. The toy we call *Buzz*, for example, used to be originally made with fresh palm leaves. Toymakers then substituted palm leaves with paper to make a longer lasting toy.

Yet despite all their innovative energy and drive, such artisans have all but disappeared. Where there were over a 100 toymakers at a typical village fair in India around 35 years ago, and perhaps an impoverished 4 or 5 even 10 years ago, you would be lucky to find even one today.

What happened to them and why did these folk toys die out? The reasons are complex, but they're linked to two basic factors: since the 1980s, a capital-intensive toy industry has flooded the market through pervasive advertising and wide distribution. This is essentially for a middle-class market. For poorer children, traditional toys have been replaced by cheap, mass-produced (and crudely made) plastic wares. Folk toymakers have had to contend with this, with no capital, either monetary or social, of their own. Hardly anyone wants their toys anymore.

Most people no longer value local knowledge or artisanship, and the loss of these things is not seen as cultural impoverishment. Mass-produced toys are standardised, 'modern', and therefore, aspirational, for those who are upwardly mobile. To this way of thinking, a folk toy is seen primarily as a poor child's plaything, meant for those who can't afford anything 'better'.

There are, of course, small efforts at reviving the dying craft, but unless larger cultural and economic factors are addressed, folk toys will remain 'ethnic' and 'exotic'. It may be too ambitious to try and resurrect this tiny dying industry, but we can revive its value and standing, by bringing these toys (and the principles behind their making) into the mainstream of children's play. It may or may not bring the toymakers back, but will definitely restore real choices in a rapidly homogenising world.

Buzz p. 10

Tradition is contemporary

Folk toys are considered 'traditional'. But what is tradition? For most people, tradition is something that is associated with the past, an unchanging way of doing things, which is handed down from generation to generation. In the simplest sense, a tradition is indeed a set of beliefs or practices inherited from the past. But in lived reality, traditions are not fixed: they change and evolve, through time, as well as through contact with outside influences. Strong traditions adapt to changing conditions, while still retaining a connection to older ways of doing things. This is how they grow. In fact, the more a tradition is willing to engage creatively with change, the more vibrant it is.

Before the advent of big capital and the toy industry, folk toymaking survived by constantly updating itself. We looked at our collection of folk toys, and to our surprise, discovered that many of them were made with recycled objects such as bottle caps, tin cans, bicycle spokes, or springs from ball-point pens. These materials don't fit in with most people's idea of tradition, and the children in our workshop asked us about this when we made the toy we call *Hip-hop*. It uses an ordinary piece of card, although the original toy was probably made from a piece of tree bark or pith.

So folk toymakers used any material they could find, in a completely unselfconscious way. As far as they were concerned, the rules on what could and couldn't be used were flexible. With many traditional raw materials no longer cheaply available to them, they simply looked around, and creatively recycled everyday material into new uses. What endured, then, was the principle behind the toy, and this is what is 'traditional' about it.

Looked at in this light, tradition can be considered a particular relationship to the past. Tradition is not the past, per se, but what links us to the past. Therefore, when artists innovate in order to stay relevant and contemporary, they do not move away from their heritage, rather, they render it pertinent to the present.

Hip-hop pg. 33

Playing with material

Most urban children today prefer to play with toys bought in shops. Earlier, in large parts of the world, children themselves would fashion many of the things they played with, making their own kites, dolls, catapults or tops. In India, youngsters in villages—or in poorer neighbourhoods in cities—still continue to put together their playthings from what is available around them. But by and large, the toy has become a product made in factories, by experts. Most children, especially those who can afford to buy toys, are consumers of ready-made products—and one of the consequences of this is a lack of imaginative involvement with the materials around them.

The ingenious possibilities in everyday material are no longer part of children's creative lives. This is something that the making of folk toys can rekindle, for each of these toys comes from an ingenious use of material at hand. The *Yankee*, for instance, has a fascinating history. It was originally made in Kerala using a hollow seed from a rubber tree. To hollow the seed out, toymakers would leave a fresh seed near an anthill, leaving the ants to eat away the pulp without damaging the hard shell.

The children in our workshop were fascinated by this story. They immediately began to think of other natural things they picked up and played with: burrs they threw on each other's clothing, milkweed seeds that exploded, floating canoes from fruit pods, winged seeds that flew...

When we came back to the hollow rubber seeds from Kerala, we pointed out that they were not available to us, so we needed to use something else instead. Our version of this traditional toy was going to be a variation, and needed intelligent substitution of material. In the event we used ping-pong balls instead of rubber seeds. This substitution exercise made us

realise how important it is to encourage children to observe and experiment with what is locally available, so that they notice and become interested in everyday material.

In our workshop, we noticed that children from poorer schools had a more attentive, playful and inventive attitude towards materials. They threw nothing away. Children from more affluent backgrounds sometimes showed disregard (even contempt) for simple things around them. It struck us as ironic that in today's world, it is only the child without means, who cannot buy and play with anything 'better', who still has the freedom to look around at what is available and see what it can be turned into. Interestingly, when artisans innovate, and look for newer material to use instead of natural materials that are not available anymore, they also tend to look around them and pick on what is thrown away.

So in our workshop, we focused particularly on materials that are considered throwaway trash—and demonstrated how these could be recycled to make interesting toys.

Yankee pg. 64

Making your own toy

We wanted to find out from the children in our workshop what they experienced making their own toys. As a case in point, we chose a simple paper whistle called *Screech*. It seemed easy enough to make and we also choose it because it was particularly hard for us to imagine how anything as noisy and potentially disruptive as *Screech* could have any pedagogical merit. So we picked this one, and asked children what they got out of making it. Here's the extraordinary list they came up with:

1. Keep trying till you get things right.

2. Don't waste even a small piece of paper.

3. Every time you blow, you get a different sound.

4. Some people buy these things made of plastic, we can make it ourselves with paper.

5. Anybody can do it.

6. You can use waste paper.

7. Couldn't you do this with leaves?

8. I felt sleepy when I blew!

9. We can make anything, if we use our imagination and we think a bit.

10. This works best in dry places.

11. Blowing on it is a strange feeling.

12. Vibration of the paper causes sound.

13. The noise is really irritating.

14. Thinner paper, more holes: lower pitch. Thicker paper, less holes: higher pitch.

15. I can make three toys from one piece of paper.

16. I can make toys with strange materials.

17. Be patient until it works.

18. Works better with three holes.

19. Keep using the paper until it wears out.

20. You can make sound with paper.

21. When you have nothing else to do or play with, you can make your own toy.

22. You learn to listen.

23. Learn science while making toys.

24. If a bought toy breaks, you can't make it again. If a toy you make breaks, you can make it again.

25. It can be given as a gift.

Screech pg. 12

The value of short-lived toys

While there are favourite toys that children return to again and again, the converse is also true. They often play with a toy for a while and then tire of it. If the toy is expensive, this can turn out to be quite dismaying for parents. Folk toys take care of such short attention spans quite simply: many of them seem to have built-in obsolescence. Made of perishable material, they are by nature short-lived. In a sense, this can actually be seen as a blessing, since it allows children to engage with the toy as long as it interests them, and then move on to something else once their curiosity has run its course.

Take the toy we call *Stitch-in-time*, for example. Originally made with baby coconuts that had fallen from trees, it used to be very common in Kerala a few decades ago. The toy worked only as long as the coconut was fresh, and stopped functioning when the coconut dried out. This short-lived plaything couldn't be produced in large numbers, and couldn't travel very far. In our version of the toy, we substituted the baby coconut with a small potato, but the nature of the toy remained the same. It stopped working when the potato shrivelled up.

We could see how the toy offered our children a very special quality of experience: intrigued by the stitching noise and the stitches on the leaf, they were free to investigate its workings by taking it apart. They could dismantle it and put it together again, and play with it until it stopped working. Some intrepid children made fresh ones immediately, while others drifted off.

Stich-in-time pg. 14

Process and product

When children are involved in creating their own playthings, many of their usual opinions and attitudes seem to fall away. The contemporary child is full of received notions on what is 'cool' and what is not. More often than not, these opinions are based on the child's sense of the right thing to say in order to belong, rather than from any lived experience. So we actually expected a number of children in our workshop (who are used to complicated high-tech toys) to be unimpressed about making noise with bits of paper. This was in effect what the toy we call *Flute-hoot* was all about. To our gratification, we turned out to be wrong.

Children were engrossed in their activity, and though the toy was simple enough to make, their excitement was centred on how to get it to work. It seemed completely unpredictable in its response. We were surprised at the learning potential this little bit of paper afforded. Making the toy consisted of learning how to roll and fold paper precisely, but the real work was in getting it to function as a hoot. You had to learn how to hold it, and blow air through it, in a very particular way. In the process, children began to acquire an intuitive understanding of material properties—of what, in more abstract terms, amounts to the attributes of paper and its relationship to the quality of the sound it makes.

We also saw children dealing with failure in positive ways. When her hoot didn't make any sound, a child looked to her neighbour: why did his toy work? She re-examined hers, stretched the paper differently, blew harder, asked for help, and then decided to remake the toy entirely. Her aim was to get it to work. When you create something, you take responsibility for it. One child said: "If you buy a toy and it doesn't work, you go and exchange it, or even throw it away. But if you've made it, you have to find out why it doesn't work and try to make it work." Precisely. The toy you make yourself is not just a product that does or does not work, but a process of which you are a part.

Flute-hoot pg. 20

Dare to be different

Increasingly, money seems to be the prime marker of value in today's culture, an attitude that children come to share all too soon. Many toys on the market are 'status toys': the more expensive the toy, the higher its perceived value. Very often, this has little to do with the possibilities it opens up. Yet, the toy industry and the media have a high stake in convincing us that expensive, beautifully packaged products are valuable in themselves. To a large extent, we are unthinking participants in a culture that persuades us not only of the primacy of money as the indicator of value, but also of homogeneity as a desirable state. We are becoming increasingly wary of standing out, and of being judged by our peers.

Last year, a friend sent us a *Hum*, a toy he had made himself, as a New Year gift. We mentioned this to the children in our workshop when we made the toy with them. But they weren't too keen on the idea of making a few to give away as presents. They said that they neither liked to give, nor receive, homemade gifts. Such presents were not 'real', unlike bought toys. This made us pause and think about the issue: even if a child is persuaded to spend time and creative energy in making a toy for a friend's birthday, how will the present be received? Will it be valued in the light of how much care, work and time it takes?

But before we engage with our children, we need to look at ourselves first, in the light of whether we question the messages we receive. Are we as afraid as our children of being different, of giving a homemade gift? Are we nervous that this will make us appear cheap? Why? To be able to talk to children about the meaning of giving and receiving gifts, we need to look critically at the prevailing culture, and see how we are part of it. To act differently takes courage and energy. But it is worth persuading a child to make a toy to give away, and to receive such gifts with the care and respect they deserve.

This kind of positive adult intervention is necessary to help children exercise real choice, and not give in to mindless consumerist or peer pressure. Market forces are naturally out to persuade us that freedom lies in an increase in the number of goods we can buy. But real freedom is the ability to make choices that are neither dictated by the marketplace nor by what everybody else is doing.

Hum pg. 22

What is true interaction?

Today, a bewildering number of toys, apps and multimedia games claim to be 'interactive'. They range in quality—some are better thought-out and put together than others, yet the operative word is always 'interactive', and most adults caring for children believe this is a good thing. So the question we asked ourselves was: how does one evaluate interactivity? What kind of interaction do these games and apps foster? And can we foster another kind of interaction, which does not involve expensive gadgets?

We tried it with a game we invented ourselves, and it involved a toy we call *Rat-a-tat*. It makes a singular noise when you pull along its knotted string, and interestingly, each toy makes a slightly different sound, depending on the way it's put together. We called our game *The Penguin Game*: it was based on the fact that a mother penguin recognises the cry of her own baby, from amongst a horde of baby penguins.

We gathered all the *Rat-a-tats* the children had made— these would substitute for Mother Penguins. We said that we would sound out each of these toys, and asked the children to pay close attention, and see if they recognised the sound of their own toy. All the *Rat-a-tats* seemed to sound alike, and we honestly didn't expect more than a few children to recognise their 'babies'. To our astonishment, almost all of them managed to recognise the sound of their own toys! And these were children who are usually told that they don't pay attention. Obviously, their quality of attention and response had a great deal to do with something they had created themselves. They knew it intimately and responded to it individually. This was true interaction.

This made us reflect again on the claim of 'interactivity' that games and app manufacturers put out, and for the need to ask some fundamental questions: how does a player interact with an app or virtual play-worlds? What is required of her? Is it mainly speed of response to solutions that are already in place? Does excelling at the game require the player only to react quickly? Or is the interaction to do with 'choice', with the options available to the player, none of which are actually defined by him? In any case, if speed is what is required, then the best response would be an almost unthinking reflex. If he has the right to 'choose', then the question would be: how much freedom does he have to make his own rules? Are there resolutions that are not part of a given scheme?

With many games like this, the better you get at it, the less attention you need to pay.

Rat-a-tat pg. 24

History through toys

The past is part of who and what we are today. Our sense of what constitutes the past is getting ever weaker, particularly with technology evolving at such a dizzying speed. Added to this is the fact that children are at a stage in their lives when they are still developing a basic sense of time. To inculcate the concept of what has gone before—such as the ones who made the toys featured in this book—is therefore important. With this in mind, we found that thinking about where toys came from, and how they develop, is a productive way to explore history. It also adds a whole new dimension to the way we—and children—think about toys.

Many toys didn't start out as toys to begin with. We discovered, for example, that our toy called *Frogodile* was based on a little device from the 18th Century that soldiers in the French army used when they marched along.

We began to read up on toy histories, and discovered that many toys have had a long history of development, not necessarily associated with childhood.

For instance, in many parts of the world, small clay figurines, root carvings and small painted animals were part of religious or everyday rituals. Some of these little figurines later became dolls and toys. We read of artefacts designed in later centuries, to provide amusement for royalty or the aristocracy. The earliest doll's houses, for instance, were Dutch cabinets filled with miniatures made in silver and other precious metals. Musical toys and tin automata with clockwork movement were created by inventors as experiments in scientific principles, and as simulations of independent life.

Some of these mechanical toys seemed to have been quite macabre, such as the 16th Century life-sized tiger of Tipu Sultan, which ate up its feebly struggling victims, while simulating real groans. The classic among mechanical toys was the legendary nightingale that appears in the Hans Andersen story

of the same name. We read out the story to our group of children, to get them started on a project to explore toy traditions and stories. On their own, during the next few days, many of the children brought in histories of toys: from their parents and grandparents, and from books they had looked up.

Frogodile pg. 17

Learning through play?

Play and learning are undoubtedly connected. There are entire systems of education, such as the Montessori method, which are based on creative learning through play. When they play with a ball, for example, young children develop co-ordination, recognition of rules and communication with others. But is that all? There is a lot more to the experience, when play is free and unstructured. During such free play, learning is not the main focus. It is incidental, and has more to do with an intangible inner movement towards understanding. The relationship between play and this kind of deep learning is complex and indirect.

We saw this at work, while making the toy we called *Jitter-bug*. A child decided to turn his bug into a snake. But the snake didn't dance down the string, as it was supposed to, it just slid down. The child continued to play with his toy, conversing with his snake, holding the toy in all kinds of ways... until suddenly the snake finally did what it was supposed to: it jerked all the way down the string. Why? The child wasn't able to articulate this precisely, but managed to figure out the principle intuitively; so much so that he managed to get the toy to work again and again. His understanding was unforced, he was just playing. Insights arrived at in this kind of tangential way almost always open up wider areas of experience.

In today's competitive environment, most parents tend to be eager that their children learn more, at an ever earlier age. Unfortunately, the kind of learning they want for their child is less about opening up wider areas: rather, it tends to be directed more towards doing better at school. Play and educational toys then become a means to this end. While parents are prepared to pay any amount for toys that they perceive as relevant to their child's future career, they forget about the other equally important kinds of play she needs.

Sadly, the child's time then begins to be structured and directed in very restrictive ways, with parents encouraging anything 'educational' and devaluing other kinds of free play. How do we evaluate so-called educational toys, games or apps? One way would be to see how far they recognise the indirect and complex relationship between activity and learning. We need to be wary of rigid approaches—such as games that merely reinforce school lessons or apps that set out to teach pre-schoolers mathematics.

Jitter-bug pg. 28

It's good to be bored

The toy we called *Clap-trap* was relatively simple to make, and we had a group of older kids who finished earlier than the time we allotted to the session. They played around with their *Clap-traps* for a while, happily startling the rest of the group with sudden noises. After they were shooed away from those still making their toy, they started to complain that they were bored. We did nothing about it, and offered them no way out. Finally, one of them came up with the idea of starting a *Clap-trap* band, with each one producing a different noise. Immediately, the bored group turned themselves into active entertainers, keeping not only themselves, but also the rest of the group engaged.

It occurred to us that there is a positive value to being truly bored. It leaves you with no choice but to find a way out of your impasse, using your own resources. Can children today actually do this? More and more, we find that every available instant is filled, either with school, organised activity, TV, or online distraction. Many adults feel that there is nothing wrong with this. Doesn't the child overburdened with school work need to relax in his leisure time?

The problem is we have lost sight of what leisure means, since every waking moment is filled. When a child is constantly occupied or entertained, he merely consumes, with little space to discover his own skills of creativity or imagination. When an activity gets boring, all he needs to do is switch to another pre-programmed one. With little need to exert himself to do anything self-generated, the child's idea of a good time is to let himself be occupied, warding off boredom at all cost.

Active play, on the other hand (particularly when it gets boring) induces the child to move off in a new, unforeseen direction. It is this quality that turns dead-end situations such as the one we had into take-off points for invention.

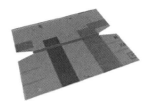

Clap-trap pg. 40

Stages of play

When we made the *Rock-n-roll* with a group of kids of different ages, we wondered whether the older ones would enjoy creating this toy meant for very young children. Their interest and involvement came as a welcome surprise to us. Our misgiving was based on the fact that children grow out of certain kinds of play. Toys in the market are graded according to age levels, and older children don't generally play with 'baby' toys. The toy industry consciously promotes this, since it increases sales. Perhaps as a result, children today 'outgrow' their toys much more rapidly than ever before.

In all this, we forget that there have always been traditional playthings (such as kites) which children of all ages have played with. They do this at varied levels of skill and complexity. There is positive value in this: various age groups can play together, but they experience it differently. Depending on age and perspective, the same experience can mean very different things.

We saw this at work when we made the *Rock-n-roll*. For young children, the excitement was in simply in making and playing with a toy that magically rocked to and fro without ever tipping over. Even though the children had made it themselves, there was still an element of wonder every time they showed it to a friend. The experience was complete in itself, it required no further explanation. Some of them listened to our scientific analysis of why the toy functioned, but didn't really take it in. Its working seemed magical, and magic is the opposite of rational explanation.

A small child's way of making sense of the world contains a lot of magical thought, and it is only when she gets older that she starts looking for more objective explanations. Unsurprisingly, how and why the toy worked was its precise fascination for older children. Here was a concrete manifestation of physics principles they had learned as abstractions in the classroom. The satisfaction was in understanding the relationship between structure and physical principles, in grasping the connection between weight, balance, and centre of gravity. Clearly, older children are interested in causation, in more realistic, logical (and sometimes sadly) more conventional ways. Solving the mystery of the *Rock-n-roll's* function was a way of making its movement more predictable and less magical.

Rock-n-roll pg. 35

Open and closed systems of play

We decided to start a story with the toy we called *Pop-up*: one child held up her toy, and came up with a sentence, and the next one took it up to move the story ahead. They created a world more delightfully bizarre than anyone could imagine, inhabited by strange characters, and leading to the most extraordinary conclusion.

It was typical of the kind of imaginative leaps most children delight in. The experience led us to think seriously about the quality of imaginative play today. When we asked the children what they liked to play with most, several of the little girls mentioned a ubiquitously popular doll. This impossibly svelte young woman had a wardrobe for every occasion and role, she liked to shop, she had a boyfriend and a best friend... we were told all this and more, including some favourite plotlines. The children's imagination was being channelled along defined paths, the designer having thought through the characters and the accessories... marketing and promotions then added further storylines.

In this kind of scenario, even though the child is theoretically free to invent her own stories, she will tend to imitate what has been laid out already, and rarely will her imagination stray too far from what she knows about the character and the story. These kinds of dolls are part of what can be called a closed system of play.

Apart from the lack of imaginative freedom, closed systems of play bring two other serious problems with them. One is the context in which a particular toy and its storyline are set. This is the world-view the child imitates, and to an extent, internalises. The sexy-plastic-pretty-ultra-feminine personality of the doll our children talked about, and the world she inhabits, capture the teenage ideals and fantasies of mainstream American society. Some of these dolls in India have her wearing Indian clothes. But this does not in any way fundamentally alter the context and assumptions she brings with her. These are problematic in themselves. But they are also from a particular society, and are not universal. Yet these dolls are marketed as if the values of mainstream American society are valid everywhere or ought to be valid everywhere. So an Indian child playing with such a doll imitates actions and relationships that are neither freely imaginative, nor really cosmopolitan in an inclusive sense.

The second problem with toys within a closed system is that they exploit children's play in a way that primarily serves the needs of the market. Products such as clothes or accessories, for instance, go with each character, and each product invariably fulfills a small specific need. Not only the key characters, but accessories that go with them are meant for a specific story. Other toys with other scenarios are needed for other play. As a result, the child who wants to participate in this play becomes an easy victim of consumerism. For children who play only with these toys, play becomes less imaginative and more imitative. Sadly, it also turns into an entirely commodity-based activity.

Pop-up pg. 45

Traditional play

We watched a group of children play with this very simple toy called *Retpocileh*: they were pretending that their creations were birds, racing each other. The excitement was more around the stories and rules they had created, rather than the toy itself, which seemed more of a prop for the game they had made up.

Traditionally, in many cultures, toys were props for play, rather than the other way around. Play came first, toys followed. Toys were made at home, out of clay or rags, which stood in for dolls, or anything else the child fancied. Many toys were made by children themselves, to meet their own ideas of play. When they played in a group, children were involved in joint activities, allocating roles, trying out ideas, disagreeing, resolving differences. They also learnt to share, take turns, cooperate and develop scripts and stories. Play was also among mixed age groups. In India, children and adults often played the same games, just like they performed the same tasks towards making a living.

The concept of childhood as something entirely separated from adulthood is a notion which arose in ninteenth century Europe. With the coming of the culture of the market, this has translated into the development of products exclusively for children, and as a consequence, the nature of play has changed. It has become more centred on commodities, and less around free interaction and participation. Many children, especially in urban India, have no time for free play. Others have no safe place, in crowded apartment blocks or busy streets.

Even when children get together, they need toys and games to play with, rather than simply with each other. In India, traditional play is still around. But only poorer children still play freely, spinning hand-made windmills and chasing old cycle tyres. This may well be because they have no choice in the matter, since they lack money to buy toys.

Retpocileh pg. 50

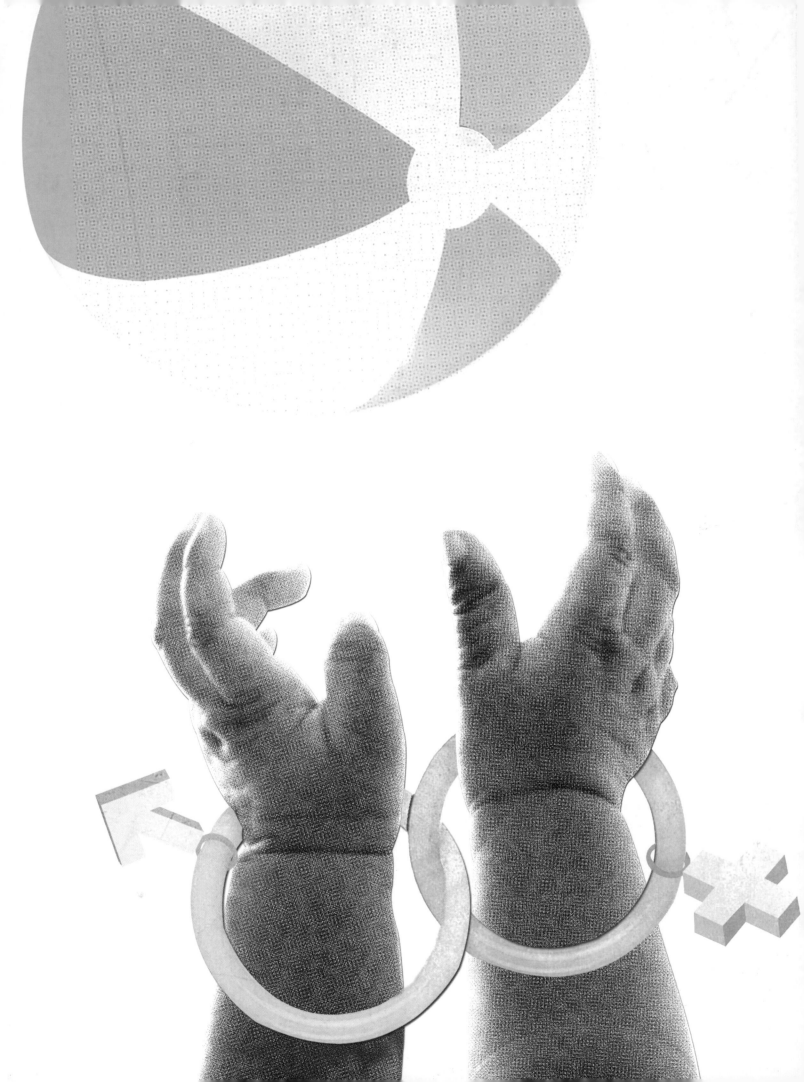

Dolls were for both sexes

The *Naf* was a toy which needed movement in order to work. While the boys in our group began to run around with their plaything as soon as they had made one, we could see the girls hesitating. A few bolder ones joined in, but by and large, they tended to be shy and sedate, and uncertain about whether they could have unabashed physical fun in the way the boys did as a matter of course. We had to actively encourage them to go ahead, and when they did, it was a pleasure to see their joy. It is not that they didn't want to run around, it was just the way they had been brought up.

We accept as a matter of course (especially in India) that boys run around actively while girls tend to sit and talk. Other cultures have their own stereotypes about how boys and girls behave, and this often goes back to even more problematic notions about how they are, innately. Even without getting deeply into the whole issue of gender stereotyping, we can say with confidence that there is more that unites the two sexes than differentiates them, especially when they are young. And that, all children, regardless of gender, have the right to different kinds of play, without being rigidly socialised into 'boys' and 'girls'.

One of the mainstays of such socialisation is through toys. This has a long history, and it is sometimes not what we would expect, seen from today's perspective. For instance in Europe, around a century-and-a-half ago, baby dolls used to be for both sexes. It was only during the late nineteenth century that playing with dolls became exclusively a girl's domain. Now it is not just society but also the toy industry which determines what boys and girls play with.

The industry does not just mirror social conventions— it actively creates them. Its ideas on gender are conservative and largely unquestioned: it began with kitchen sets for girls, and toy soldiers for boys. Over time, this bias has taken an even more regressive turn, and many toys today extoll male violence and female sex appeal in more extreme forms. Macho and action-oriented toys for boys are matched by toys for girls with an emphasis on domesticity, fashion and physical appearance. Disturbingly, this gendering is happening for ever younger age groups. There are even some baby toys marked with the objectionable blue or pink tag.

It's no surprise when this form of early socialisation turns out to be a self-fulfilling prophecy: boys will turn out to be outward looking, and girls will be demure. The solution does not lie merely in exchanging playthings. We need new kinds of toys: not only those which grant mobility and adventure to girls, or allow boys to fantasise about relationships, but also more toys that are gender-neutral, for both boys and girls. All children, regardless of their gender, need to experience various kinds of play: physical, imaginative, quiet, exuberant, solitary and social. To divide these needs into innate boy and girl oppositions is to deny an individual child the freedom and right to a range of play.

Naf pg. 56

Changing the rules of the game

The *Huff-n-puff* was the kind of toy that invited challenges. Groups of children devised games with their toys, some with relatively simple rules, such as seeing who could blow their bead up highest. Others went on to evolve more complicated scenarios, with teams keeping score of how many times the bead could be made to hop up and down. Rules kept changing constantly. There was a lot of bickering, negotiation and compromise.

When play is turned into a game, a set of rules has to be defined, and all the players have to keep to them. Children need to be part of this kind of decision-making as a group, to be able to evolve (as well as change) the rules of the game. Do the kind of games children play these days encourage a sense of democratic participation? Who makes these rules and what are they? Are they the ones we expect our children to adhere to?

We found that some simple outdoor games (such as hide and seek, or marbles) allow a flexible and creative framing of new rules. Classical as well as newer board games had more well-defined rules, with some amount of mutual negotiation possible. Games set in specific contexts had their own problems, many of them to do with issues of money, and unquestioning social values: we found a doctor set that let the child operate only on one particular organ. The winner of the game was the one who managed to charge the most fees for an operation. We also looked at complex board games based on adult situations such as career, marriage, or car insurance—and here again the play options tended to reinforce questionable social stereotypes, where the player needs to pay for a 'son's education' or 'a daughter's marriage'.

Popular online games and apps canbe just as limiting, though their technical wizardry might make it seem that there is more that children can actually do, by way of choosing and steering a game or a scenario. And yet the question remains: can a child user step outside the framework and come up with her own rules?

So the creative freedom to question any of the givens remains one of the most valuable aspects of traditional play.

Huff-n-puff pg. 60

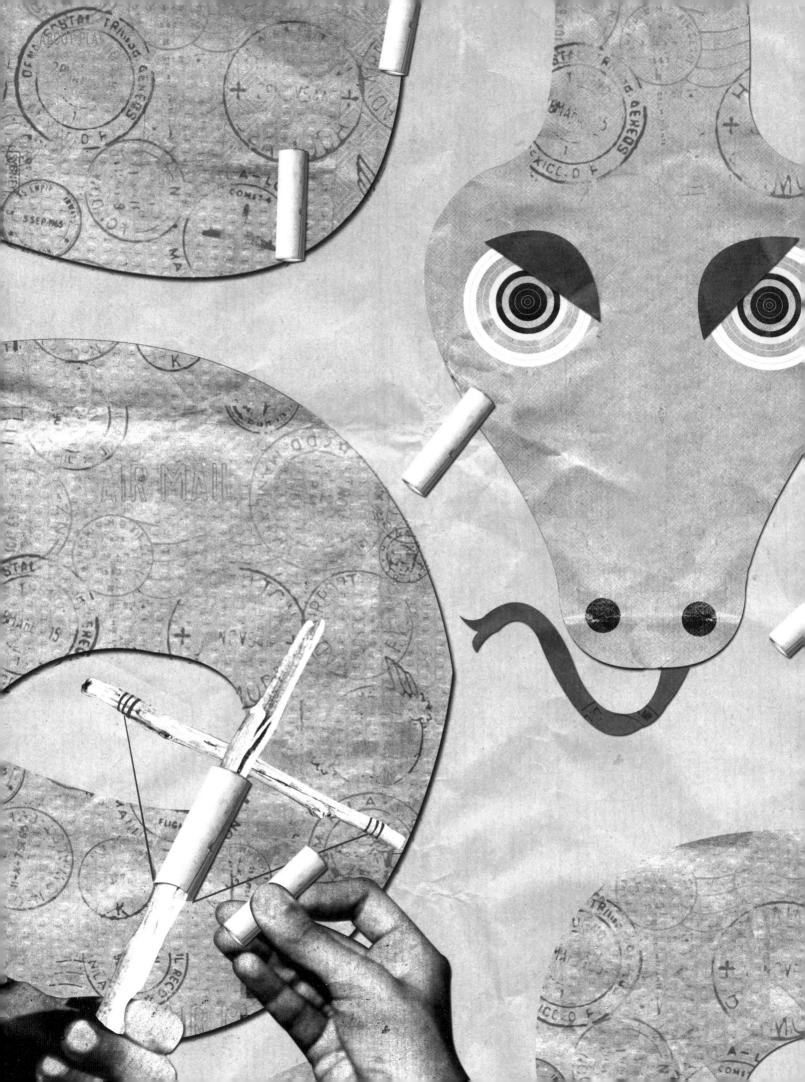

Violent toys

As soon as they had finished making the *Shoot-a-reel*, a group of noisy children trained their toys at others nearby, chasing them around the room and threatening to shoot them dead. Did we have only ourselves to blame for unleashing this spate of violence, by helping rowdy children make a potential weapon? But when we looked around, we saw to our relief that not everyone was doing this. Other groups were using their toys differently: some were practicing shooting at targets, and others were firing them in the air, pretending they were rockets. The *Shoot-a-reel* was a very dynamic toy, and certainly not something that induced children to play quietly—the chances that it could be used in aggressive ways was admittedly high. Was this something to be discouraged on principle?

Most people believe that playing with violent toys causes no lasting harm: such play helps children fantasise and let off latent aggression. There is something to this argument. Most of us have played games like 'Police and Robbers' with toy guns as children, to no ostensible harm and have matured into relatively peace-loving adults. But the 21st Century seems to be at another level altogether, and popular culture is full of very disturbing trends. Children today are bombarded with unbelievable levels of blood-thirstiness through films, television, war toys and video games, at a very young age. What is more, violence is often presented as pure style: a 'cool' trope which glamourises brutality and de-sensitises the child to the harm that real brutality causes. This kind of environment naturally influences the stories that children act out with their toys.

In addition to this, a toy whose purpose is clearly pre-programmed (say a machine gun) already has violence built into its playscript. You shoot down people or animals with a gun. A toy weapon translates into obvious use, making it harder for the child to do something completely different with it.

And we would argue that these kinds of violent toys not only channel children's fantasies in aggressive ways, their macho image also contributes to extreme gender stereotyping.

So to come back to our *Shoot-a-reel*: it is essentially not like a toy weapon you can buy. It could be put to potentially violent uses, but its basically open-ended form does not necessarily insist on being used in one particular way. The manner in which various children played with it had more to do with their own inclinations: one child in fact put wings on to the reel and launched birds into flight.

There was also something else going on here: while a child is absorbed in making the toy, his creative energy is completely engaged in getting the thing to work. How to use it then becomes a much more open-ended question, because in most cases, the playing out of violent stories is less likely to capture the child who needs to pay careful attention to creating something.

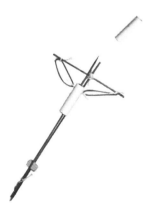

Shoot-a-reel pg. 69

What is a good toy?

The *Flutter-fly* was one of the simplest toys we made, but it opened up a surprising number of ideas and possibilities. Some children had a race with their toys, others tried to make it move on different surfaces. Some experimented with breathing and blowing. The older ones were intrigued with the science behind the movement of the *Flutter-fly*, which was very complex in contrast to the actual simplicity of the toy. Such toys can be considered seeds that contain the relationship between many things: science, technology, material, design, and cultures of play. Anything, in fact, can be a toy, if we choose to describe what we do with it as play. And going by the experience of the children in our workshop, the *Flutter-fly* had high play value.

Children today are faced with an overabundance of choice when it comes to toys. Given peer pressure as well as the relentless marketing of products to children, adults find themselves stressed by the demands of the children in their care. In India, as in other parts of the world, there are any number of wealthy parents who think the latest thing in the market and all that money can buy is best for their child. We need to be wary of succumbing mindlessly to every novelty the toy industry puts out and exhorts the child to possess.

Some of these 'new' toys have very doubtful value. They are status objects for their owners, used for a short while before they are discarded when the next thing comes along. Children cannot be expected to resist such an onslaught on their own. They need adult support and guidance when they decide to buy toys for themselves or their friends. Apart from the necessity of learning to say no to every request from a child, when we do decide to buy a toy, how do we judge its play value?

We thought up a broad list of guidelines:

1. Expensive toys need not necessarily be the best in terms of play value.

2. A toy, which is part of a very specific context, needing many ready-made accessories, is short-lived and geared towards consumerism. Does the toy also bring in values you do not wish to endorse (status, money)? Does it come with a strong storyline already in place?

3. Examine educational toys carefully: does your child really need that kind of pressure?

4. What experiences does the toy offer in terms of creative participation or imaginative possibilities?

5. Is the toy slotted as for a 'boy' or 'girl'? Do you wish to endorse this kind of gender stereotyping at an early age?

6. Does it foster violence?

Flutter-fly pg. 52

Appendix

Centrifugal Force (pg. 32, 63)

An object travelling in a circle behaves as if it is experiencing an outward force. This force, known as the centrifugal force, depends on the mass of the object, the speed of rotation, and the distance from the center. Expressed as a formula,

$$F_c = \frac{mv^2}{r}$$

Here the centrifugal force (F_c) is proportional to the mass of the object (m), the speed in which it is rotating (v) and inversely proportional to the radius along which it acts.

Centre of Gravity (pg. 37, 53)

The centre of gravity (CoG) of an object is the point at which weight is evenly dispersed and all sides are in balance. The Centre of Gravity determines the stability of an object. A bottom heavy object like the Rock-n-roll in Page 37 is stable because it has a low centre of gravity.

Centre of Lift (pg. 53)

The centre of lift (CoL) is the point where the sum total of all lift generated by parts (principally by wings, control surfaces, and other fuselage parts) balances out and the aggregate direction their force will act on a craft while in an atmosphere. For the object to fly with some stability, the CoL is generally on the same line as CoG.